Native American Religions

The Religious Life of Man Series
FREDERICK J. STRENG, *SERIES EDITOR*

Texts

Understanding Religious Life, Second Edition
    Frederick J. Streng

The House of Islam, Second Edition
    Kenneth Cragg

Japanese Religion: Unity and Diversity, Third Edition
    H. Byron Earhart

Chinese Religion: An Introduction, Third Edition
    Laurence G. Thompson

The Christian Religious Tradition
    Stephen Reynolds

The Buddhist Religion, Third Edition
    Richard H. Robinson and Willard L. Johnson

The Way of Torah: An Introduction to Judaism, Third Edition
    Jacob Neusner

The Hindu Religious Tradition
    Thomas J. Hopkins

Native American Religions: An Introduction
    Sam D. Gill

Anthologies

The Chinese Way in Religion
    Laurence G. Thompson

Religion in the Japanese Experience: Sources and Interpretations
    H. Byron Earhart

The Buddhist Experience: Sources and Interpretations
    Stephan Beyer

The Life of Torah: Readings in the Jewish Religious Experience
    Jacob Neusner

Islam from Within
    Kenneth Cragg and Marston Speight

Native American Religions
An Introduction

Sam D. Gill

Arizona State University

Wadsworth Publishing Company
Belmont, California
A Division of Wadsworth, Inc.

Religion Editor: Sheryl Fullerton
Production Editor: Diane Sipes
Art Director: Detta Penna
Designer: Christopher Werner
Copy Editor: John Eastman
Illustrator: Valerie Martino

Library of Congress Cataloging in Publication Data

Gill, Sam D., 1943–
    Native American religion.

    (Religious life of man series)
    Includes index.
    1. Indians of North America—Religion and
    mythology.
I. Title.
E98.R3G48   299'.78   80-28134

ISBN 0-534-00973-5

Printed in the United States of America

1 2 3 4 5 6 7 8 9 10 — 86 85 84 83 82

for Jennifer Robin

Contents

Illustrations

Foreword

THE RELIGIOUS LIFE OF MAN series is intended as an introduction to a large complex field of inquiry—human religious experience. It seeks to present the depth and richness of religious concepts, forms of worship, spiritual practices, and social institutions found in the major religious traditions throughout the world.

As a specialist in the languages and cultures in which a religion is found, each author is able to illuminate the meanings of a religious perspective and practice in a community. To communicate this meaning to readers who have had no special training in these cultures and religions, the authors have attempted to provide clear, nontechnical descriptions and interpretations of religious life.

Different interpretive approaches have been used, depending upon the nature of the religious data; some religious expressions, for example, lend themselves more to developmental, others more to topical studies. But this lack of a single interpretation may itself be instructive, for the experiences and practices regarded as religious in one culture may not be the most important in another.

The Religious Life of Man is concerned with, on the one hand, the variety of religious expressions found in different traditions and, on the other, the similarities in the structures of religious life. The various forms are interpreted in terms of their cultural context and historical continuity, demonstrating both the diverse expressions and commonalities of religious traditions. Besides the single volumes on different religions, the series offers a core book on the study of religious meaning, which describes different study approaches and examines several modes and structures of religious awareness. In addition, each book presents a list of materials for further reading, including translations of religious texts and detailed examinations of specific topics.

During a decade of use the series has experienced a wide readership. A continuing effort has been made to update the scholarship, simplify the organization of material, and clarify concepts through the publication of revised editions. The authors have been gratified with the response to their efforts to introduce people to various forms of religious life. We hope readers will also find these volumes "Introductory" in the most significant sense: an introduction to a new perspective for understanding themselves and others.

Frederick J. Streng
Series Editor

Preface

THERE IS AND HAS BEEN among Americans and some Europeans a deep interest in Native Americans, their cultures and religions. Native American cultures are familiar to most Americans, being widely treated in literature, art, and film. Native Americans are inseparable from the American identity—its peoples, landscapes, arts, and history, and it is commonly recognized that rituals, ceremonials, and mythological stories are an important part of Native American cultures.

Few Americans would disagree that the history of the European-American encounter with Native Americans is a national dishonor and that to avoid further error on this path we must completely reshape the terms of the relationship. The basic terms must include less presumption about and more sensitivity to the world views and religious values of the Native American peoples themselves. President John F. Kennedy spoke precisely to this point when he said, "It seems a basic requirement to study the history of our Indian people. America has much to learn about the heritage of our American Indians. Only through this study can we as a nation do what must be done if our treatment of the American Indians is not to be marked down for all time as a national disgrace."[1]

Perhaps with the importance of that heritage in mind, and recognizing that religion is so essential to that heritage, the U.S. Congress passed a bill that was signed into law in 1978, establishing as the policy of the United States "to protect and preserve for American Indians their inherent right of freedom to believe, express, and exercise the traditional religions . . . including but not limited to access to sites, use and possession of sacred objects, and the freedom to worship through ceremonials and traditional rites" (Public Law 95–341).

The importance of the Native American heritage is reflected in the great ethnographic effort begun in the 19th century that produced an unprecedented record of Native American cultures. A large portion of this record concerns what we would ordinarily consider the religious aspects of culture.

As a student of religion, I have been perplexed by the issue that these factors raise. With widespread public interest, with unprecedented resources including enormous amounts among living Native Americans, with the inseparability of Native American cultures from the very identity of America, with presidential proclamations and federal laws, it is difficult to understand why systematic attention to Native American religions has yet to find a substantial place in the academic study of religion. The fact that not a single center or chair for the study of Native American religions exists in an American university bespeaks a great lack.

The fields of anthropology, linguistics, and folklore, among others, have developed and matured throughout the century as a large number of scholars have devoted themselves to studying various aspects of Native American cultures. While there is no counterpart in religious studies, students of religion have benefited from the theoretical developments in these other fields of study. Religion is clearly a dimension of Americanist studies, but it remains undeveloped.

In writing this book, my foremost goal has been to provide an introduction to Native American religions, focusing on cultures of North America. The aim is not so much to introduce data and facts as to introduce an academically and humanistically useful way of trying to appreciate and understand the complexity and diversity of Native American religions. This approach is detailed in the prologue and first three chapters of this book. I have also examined aspects of European-American history in a search for the sources of widespread misunderstandings about the character of Native American religions (even to the point of considering them unworthy of academic study). My second goal, then, is to help establish Native American religions as a significant field within religious studies. I believe that these two goals are inseparable and interdependent.

The approach I have chosen in writing this book has not allowed me to be absent from the text. Many of the issues discussed have been actualized through my own experiences, and I have chosen to present them as such. The many interpretations I have suggested are also based on premises that I have accepted. This is not to suggest, however, that my own interpretations or premises are the only valid ones.

Finally this book intends to address neither Native Americans nor non-Native Americans exclusively but all who are interested in the subject. While realizing that those Native Americans whose religions I have tried to interpret may find my interpretations either unnecessary or inadequate, I feel that the significance and value of religious acts and events are not self-evident to people outside the performing tradition; and that a need for interpretation therefore exists. I hope that the people whose religions I have presented will find them accurately presented, for the core of my interests has been to do so. Also important is that in many Native American religious traditions (as in most religious traditions), certain acts and items of information are kept from the public, even within the particular culture. I have never attempted to acquire this kind of information, and anything that I have suspected as possibly of that character I have omitted.

This book has been a pleasure to write, and I want to thank Frederick J. Streng for inviting me to write it. His measured criticism and suggestions have been most valuable. During the last several years, my discussions with Thomas W. Overholt and David Carrasco have informed and shaped this book in many ways; I thank them for this as well as for careful readings and comments on the manuscript. Judy, my wife, shared with me many of the experiences that helped formulate the approach and substance of this book. As a partner in this respect, she also gave many helpful suggestions in her several readings of the manuscript, and I want to thank her. Valerie Martino's illustrations contribute valuably, and I thank her for applying her talent to this subject. I wish also to acknowledge Jonathan Z. Smith, who has influenced my approach to the study of religion and who continues to inspire me in the pursuit of this field. Some aspects of my study of Navajo religion first appear in this book, and I want to acknowledge support of that research by Arizona State University faculty research grants. Some of the technical aspects of preparing the manuscript for publication were supported by a grant from the Lilly Endowment, Inc. I would also like to thank the following reviewers for their constructive comments: Henry Warner Bowden, of Douglass College, Rutgers University; and Alfonso Ortiz, of the University of New Mexico. Finally I want to thank all of the Native Americans who have shared their culture and traditions with me and my family.

NOTES

1. John F. Kennedy, introduction to Alvin M. Josephy, ed., *The American Heritage Book of Indians* (New York: American Heritage, 1961), p. 7.

Prologue

Before beginning this introduction to Native American religions, it is essential to place both the subject matter and my approach in the appropriate historical context. This historical context has played a major role in the understanding of Native Americans and their religions throughout the nearly 500 years of European contact. To ignore this historical background would be to pretend that we can "see" the subject matter both more clearly and on different terms than I think possible. To ignore the effects of involvement by non–Native Americans in the subject would not only be misleading; it would be a major deterrent to our sincere attempt to understand.

Therefore, instead of beginning with the earliest archeological evidence of Native American religions and developing our study from that origin, I will begin even earlier (not in a temporal but in a logical sense) by considering the ideas and images that have shaped our perceptions and conceptions of Native Americans and their religions—ideas and images fostered by the earliest stages of European contact. From this approach, we may learn why it has seemed so important for us to locate Native American origins geographically and temporally, when Native Americans themselves do not even care to consider our findings; and why we have classified an aspect of their lives as religion, when they don't seem to make such a segmentation.

ORBIS TERRARUM: THE ISLAND OF THE EARTH

In 1492 "Columbus sailed the ocean blue" on the appointed task of sailing westward around the globe until he found the east coast of Asia. In Europe at that time, it was believed that the world was composed of the three continents Europe, Asia, and Africa—all joined to form a large *Orbis Terrarum*, or Island of the Earth. This island, though positioned on a globe, was surrounded by the seas, which confined the land and gave it boundaries, limitations, and definition. The seas were associated with death, chaos, and mystery, for they stood beyond the defined earth. Furthermore, the Christian beliefs prevailing at that time in Europe held that God had created one world and that all peoples in that world were descendants of Adam and Eve.

It is in the context of this cosmology, this view of the structure of the universe, that we must place Christopher Columbus on that fine October day in 1492 when he sighted the land he believed to be the east coast of the Island of the Earth. What else could it have been? He knew what the lands and people were supposed to be like from the accounts of Marco Polo and others who had been there. Although his observations did not correspond to their accounts, in his own mind he had accomplished what he had set out to do. Each of his three subsequent voyages was made to confirm what he found with what he expected. Each time, however, the facts he collected presented more evidence that proved inconsistent with his expectations. Yet even after four voyages and considerable consternation at these discrepancies, Columbus remained solidly of one mind.

Let us look more closely at two observational aspects of these early voyages—the lands and the peoples—in order to clarify what was taking place.

On Columbus's third voyage in 1498, he had decided to sail farther south than before in order to find the lower end of the Golden Chersonese (Malay Peninsula)—which would, he believed, reveal the passage to the Indian Ocean. He landed in a gulf in what is presently Venezuela. He wanted to consider this an island near the passage to the Indian Ocean, but the water in the gulf was fresh, not salt. He was forced to recognize that he had landed not on a small island, but on a land mass of continental magnitude. This raised for him a major problem, because Marco Polo and others who had journeyed to Asia through the Indian Ocean had reported that nothing but open sea lay to the south of the Golden Chersonese. Columbus found himself having to explain not only to others, but to himself, the existence of this great land mass he had found. This was the more difficult because of the religious belief in one God-created world. To suggest that another "world" existed would be heresy; that is, a declaration of the existence of some world not of God's creation. His dilemma was resolved only by suggesting that this land was the lost paradise wherein lay the Garden of Eden, which the ancients had reported to be "at the end of the East." This decision permitted him to hold to his belief that the lands to the north that he had charted—that is, the southern coasts of the islands now known as Haiti/Santo Domingo and Cuba—were part of the mainland of Asia.

The voyage of Amerigo Vespucci (1501–1502) charted much of the east coast of South America and confirmed the great size of this "new world." He too was unable to give it identity because of the cosmological expectations of his time. While both Columbus and Vespucci referred to it as a new world, they meant the world referred to by the ancients, and thus a world created by God.

Not until 1507, when the data collected from these voyages produced a shift in the very conception of the shape and nature of the world, could these findings become fully meaningful and acceptable to Europeans. The resolution to the situation was first stated in the *Cosmographiae Introductio* published by the Academy of St. Dié. It maintained that the world was still one but that a fourth part had been found. It differed from the other parts in its characteristic features; they were continents, but this "fourth part" was an island surrounded by the sea. The extensive use of Vespucci's information apparently led to the naming of the island as "America," the feminine form of Amerigo, corresponding with the feminine names Europe and Asia.

As Edmundo O'Gorman has so brilliantly shown, these facts amount to a quite different understanding of events than historians have given us. Instead of attributing to Columbus the "discovery" of America, a position that O'Gorman shows is finally impossible to reconcile with what is known, we must recognize that America wasn't *discovered* at all; it was *invented!* In light of the late 15th-century beliefs, there was no basis for speculating even the possible existence of a continent separate from *Orbis Terrarum*. To have thought so, let alone to proclaim its discovery, was not even a possibility to the minds of Columbus and Vespucci. The land about which these and other explorers gathered data had no acceptable identity or reality to Europeans apart from its designation as the east coast of Asia until the gathered facts led to the invention of the idea of a "fourth part" of the world. This invention was the result of the constructive extension and transformation of the cosmology believed at the time—and it was a religious invention at that. The notion of invention is necessary simply because one cannot "discover" what one cannot even imagine as a possibility.[1]

This gives us insight into the second observational aspect of these explorers: the peoples they met on these lands.

Columbus called the peoples he saw *"los Indios,"* a term apparently used at the time to refer to all peoples east of the Indus River. It comes to us in English as "the Indians." To make such a designation simply placed or identified these peoples as among the known descendants of Adam and Eve. To have identified them otherwise would have been impossible, for it was believed that all human beings descended from God's initial creation. In the most general sense, Columbus had little choice; the only other possibility was not to see them as people at all, an alternative some people accepted in the early 16th century. At another level, it was a "we/they" designation: "we" are Europeans, and "they" are Indians, a people of east Asia.

But the invention of America, the designation of a "fourth part" of the world, did not resolve the problem of identifying the peoples on this "fourth part." While they had to be descendants of Adam and Eve and their designation as *"los Indios"* held, for they lived east of the Indus River, the remaining problem was how they had come to occupy the lands of America. By 1535, the Spanish historian Gonzalo Fernandez de Oviedo had already postulated the existence of a narrow sea passage, the forerunner of our present theory of migration across the Bering Strait.[2]

I have often wondered why the theories of the "origin" of Native Americans always conclude with the point of contact in Asia—or, though less often accepted, in Europe or Africa. Why do we trace the history of Native Americans backward in time and space only to their point of departure from the "Old World" and stop there? My curiosity may now be satisfied, for there is a religious motivation behind this, rooted in the late 15th- and early 16th-century beliefs in the unity of humankind. Although their premises are now stated in humanistic terms, archaeologists and anthropologists have been working on the old theological problem created by *los Indios,* and the best solution has been and still is in the establishment of a kinship connection between Native American peoples and any peoples of the other three parts of the world.

Given this historical background, the term "Indian" is not a "white invention," as Robert Berkhofer has recently called it,[3] but the application of common terminology used in the early 16th-century Christian world to designate peoples of the Far East. From that perspective, the term is wholly accurate in its application to Native Americans. This brings us to a position where we can see that the application of the term "Indian" to the native peoples of America is similar to Columbus's belief that he had found the western route to Asia. Through four voyages he saw only what the terms of his expectations and world view permitted him to see. The present-day use of the term "Indian" is much the same, for our observations of and about the peoples we have called by that name are almost wholly shaped by our assumptions and expectations. We, like Columbus, cannot possibly see what may be the most obvious facts about these peoples and their ways because such facts do not fit the terms of our beliefs.

Thus the study of "Indians" is, on the basis I have argued, actually more a study of European views toward the native peoples of America. And since this often reveals more about Europeans than about Native Americans, it is more the concern of European and European-American history. Still, since our present data and categories of understanding are so shaped by the European idea of the "Indian," let us discuss it briefly.

To extend further the parallel between our task and the situation of the world in Columbus's time, we can see that what is needed now is another *invention*—in this case, of a term that will free us from the blinding tyranny of our old term "Indian." The term "Native American" has recently come into widespread, though somewhat confused, use; but it too is fettered by expectations and assumptions, as we shall see. Yet this term nicely parallels the invention of "America," and I will continue to use it in this book in place of "Indian." The only exception relates to a very important matter that we will take up in the last chapter, the present widespread use of the term "Indian" by those I am calling "Native Americans."[4]

By using the term "Native American," I wish to signal the desire to embark upon an understanding of the peoples native to America with fewer, or at least different, expectations than those most often held heretofore; that is, I wish to acknowledge the fact that we may not actually know where we are in terms of understanding these peoples. In that admission, however, we can get on with the business of trying to see and hopefully to understand these peoples anew.

ALL MANKIND IS ONE

In mid-August 1550, the "Council of the Fourteen" met in Valladolid at the summons of Charles V of Spain to hear arguments presented by two men on matters dealing with the conquest of the New World and to decide upon the issues debated.[5] On the first day, the Renaissance scholar Juan Gines de Sepúlveda gave a three-hour presentation of his case. The next day his opponent, a Dominican who had spent some 45 years in the New World, Bartolomé de Las Casas, began presenting his position; he continued for five days, reading only parts of extensive treatises he had prepared. The issue to be decided was how to Christianize the "Indians." The arguments hinged on what manner of beings were these people so that their capacity for receiving Christianity and European civilization might be determined. Sepúlveda's position was based upon the histories of the New World, primarily those written by Gonzalo Fernandez de Oviedo, which portrayed a very negative image of these peoples. Sepúlveda linked this image with Aristotle's definition of natural slavery in order to argue that the "Indians" were slaves by nature. This position advocated the system of *encomiendaro*, which permitted colonists to use the natives for their own profit as well as to use acts of war and violence to conquer the people so that they might be Christianized.

Las Casas refuted Sepúlveda's arguments tirelessly and with extensive data, much of which was drawn from his almost half-century of experience among peoples of the New World. He attempted to show that they were a noble people developed in the arts, in language, and in government; that they were gentle and eager to learn; and that they were even quick to accept Christianity.

Though the council took up both sides of the argument and debated considerably, it finally decided on the side of Sepúlveda, though with some dissent.

Leading up to this famous event is a history of debate over the nature of the "Indians" that began before America was invented, commencing with the beginning of colonization in the late 15th century. During the first half of the 16th century, the issue had been much discussed and, according to the insightful analysis of Lewis Hanke, the debate had split into two camps. One side viewed the "Indian" as a "dirty dog," the other as a "noble savage."[6]

Our interest in recounting this early debate is to illustrate the nature of the dynamics involved from 1500 to the present in formulating the images of Native Americans. We can gain further understanding of the situation by recasting the opposing views of Sepúlveda and Las Casas into the terms of a "we/they" relationship.[7] Sepúlveda saw his own culture ("we") as Christian, civilized, learned, and advanced in the arts and production of material goods. And for Sepúlveda, the "Indians" ("they") were a perfect counterimage: pagan, uncivilized, incapable of learning, unable to govern themselves, beastly and inhumane, barbarian. In short, "they" were fit by their nature only to be slaves to Europeans. Las Casas, citing Scripture, took a stance on the basis of his religious convictions and maintained that all humankind is one by the fact of God's single creation. "He hath made of one blood all nations of men for to dwell on all the face of the earth."[8] Hence "we" are human, and "they" are human. Further, he held to the high status of their nobility and went to great lengths to demonstrate their likeness to Europeans in humanity, civility, ability to learn, and artistry. Hence for Las Casas, the only difference was that "we" are Christian and "they" are not. It became his lifework to bring Christianity to them, thus resolving any distinction at all. And he insisted that Christianity be brought to them without violence, enslavement, or mistreatment.

It is not only significant that these two men came to represent two sides of an issue debated throughout much of the 16th century but also, to an extent, that they still represent the major positions from which images of Native Americans are created. And even as Sepúlveda won the debate over Las Casas, the successors to his position have tended to be the more dominant throughout the last four centuries. We will discuss this tendency further; but first let us observe certain similarities between these positions.

Even though the earliest explorers, colonists, and historians noted differences between the native tribes they encountered in terms of their physical structure, food habits, skin color, and friendliness or hostility, the image of the "Indian" had a unitary character. Even as it became known that many different tribes, languages, and ways of life existed, Native Americans continued to be labeled under the single concept "Indians." We continue to maintain this appellation of unity by referring to the tribal designation as a "species" variety of the "genus Indian." Even after Las Casas's 50 years of contact, the variety of his data gave way to the creation of a singular image of the "Indian" as a noble savage.

We must briefly consider the significance of this unitary concept, for it applies to our invention of the term "Native American" as much as to "Indian." There are two relatively clear reasons for the steadfast insistence upon subjugating the observed variety of peoples and types to a stereotypical image.

The first reason concerns the very nature of "we/they" relationships. The relationship itself requires that "we" identify the characteristics that distinguish "us" from "them." This process encourages self-understanding or self-definition, and we can see it operating in 16th-century Europe. Owing to the developments in communication resulting from the invention of the printing press in the late 15th century and from more extensive travel, the sense of a general European identity was growing. The colonization of America was also utilized to help make the character of the "European" distinct by the foil provided in the image of the "Indian." Simply stated, many Europeans followed the argument of Sepúlveda by seeing what they needed to see in the New World—a counterimage to their view of themselves.

The second factor involved in this unity of image is the failure to distinguish between biological and cultural classifications. Cultures were designated by a defining image, as biological species were defined by a set of distinctive features. This is just as clear in identifying an image of the "European" as in creating an image of the "Indian." The confusing and blending together of national character, race, and culture led to the stereotypical images of nations and continents that remained unchallenged until the 20th century; and we continue to live with this heritage.[9]

To return now to the positions of our Spanish debaters, we probably still see Native Americans largely in the same terms as they did, and our image has doubtless been closer to that of Sepúlveda than to Las Casas. In order to free ourselves of that image, we need to identify more clearly how it has shaped the way we see. The worst aspect of the image is that it is scarcely based on observation at all but rather is simply created as a counterimage of what we consider to be our own high ideals of humanity. Thus we have placed certain expectations upon Native Americans simply by the image of them that we maintain; and these expectations seem to be always in terms of a contrast with what we admire. There is even a forcing of images when "Indians" are viewed as admirable in contrast to a disenchanting view of European-American values and ways of life. One of the most far-reaching results of our image of Native Americans is created by contrasting that image with the espoused European admiration of history, of embracing and engineering change in the form of progress. The counterimage thus thrust upon Native Americans is that of a people who are timeless and ahistorical, changeless and nonprogressive. Consequently we believe and insist that Native Americans act according to this image, even though it violates all observed facts. We tend to judge how "real" a Native American is on the basis of how close he or she comes to our image, which projects back to precontact times. This image shapes our expectations about dress, about places of residence, about language, about social activities, about nearly every aspect of their way of life. The tribe or individual who does not measure up to that timeless image is somehow, in this view, not "really Indian."

Similarly, since the image of Native Americans serves as a counterimage for civilization, we cannot permit them to enter civilization without, of course, changing their identities. The relationships of government and religious institutions to Native Americans have been greatly shaped by this image, for these relationships have been based upon an assumption that "they" are "culturally deprived" and that "we" must approach them as guardians and philanthropists.[10]

Finally and most importantly to our present concern, the counterimage we have created for the "Indian" is that of pagan or heathen, which we construe as meaning those without religion. In describing the first Native Americans whom Columbus briefly encountered, he wrote that "they do not hold any creed nor are they idolaters";[11] and Vespucci wrote, "They have no church, no religion and are not idolaters."[12] Even though the facts are overwhelmingly in contrast to the view that Native Americans have no religions, our image blinds us to these facts. According to our image, Native Americans are not supposed to have religions, at least in any terms comparable to Western religions. It is noteworthy that until very recently, American religious historians have totally avoided even mentioning Native American religions and have included "Indians" in American religion only in relationship to Christian missionization.[13]

While perhaps we can gain no understanding of Native Americans without some image of "them," we can certainly examine our image and reshape it in order to permit seeing the facts in a different light. To do so would be to enter a much-needed new phase in this history of encounter. In reconstructing this image, I think that, on the one hand, we have no choice but to hold to the conviction of Las Casas that "all mankind is one"; otherwise the subject would be merely an interest in peculiarities and oddities. But we can no longer ground this proposition on the specific religious doctrines of Christianity; rather it must be based upon anthropological and humanistic presuppositions about the universal nature of humankind. On the other hand, however, we must reject the notion of a stereotypical image argued by Las Casas and the simple, unified identity of Native Americans. While all human beings have certain capacities and characteristics in common, the expression of these may vary greatly; and we must be sensitive to that variety among Native Americans, both in the diversity of the many peoples and tribes and in the diversity of individuals within these groups. We will learn much more about certain aspects of the nature of being human by considering the significance of these varieties and differences than by distilling out only the similarities.

Of course the aspect of human nature that will be our focus is religion; and we must now consider religion as it relates to Native American cultures.

HOMO RELIGIOSUS

Introducing the term "religion" as an aspect of Native American life brings us face-to-face with many difficulties. The term's origins lie in Western, not Native American, history, and the academic study of religion remains largely of interest only to Western institutions. Only in the last century has religion been very generally accepted as a study relevant to the nature of humankind. And only in the last couple of decades has the distinction between teaching the doctrines of religion and teaching about religion as an aspect of humanity been partially clarified and accepted so that it can be legally taught in state-supported colleges and universities. This acceptance signals that our understanding of the term "religion" is undergoing considerable, even radical, changes. Thus we have difficulty defining the term that names our principal category of study.

Other difficulties arise in terms of using the word "religion" to designate an aspect of Native American life. We have difficulty finding words in Native American languages that approximate "religion." This means at the least that what we understand as religion is not linguistically distinguished in the same way by Native Americans. Furthermore, since the word "religion" has often been used in a very narrow way by ethnographers, missionaries, and government agencies from the time of Columbus, many Native Americans have often abhorred the use of the word. They associate it with the grossest of European misunderstandings of their cultures and with the most flagrant violations of their privacy and way of life. We cannot continue to ignore these difficulties and objections.

To learn a bit more from Columbus's era, we can recall that he considered religion to be equal to "creed and church," as did Vespucci. They equated religion and Christianity; and while they probably did not expect to find Christianity among "Indians," they appeared to expect some corruption of "religion" in the form of idolatry. Yet they reported finding not even that. For them, Native Americans had nothing that resembled religion. What we mean by the term "religion" is crucial to whether or not we will find that Native Americans have religions. The generally accepted proposition that underlies the study of religion as a general human phenomenon is that religion is a characteristic distinctive of human beings, that humans are by their nature religious. From one point of view, that is, we are *homo religiosus*. When we link this with our proposition that all humankind is one, we must propose that Native Americans are also religious. This complicates our ability to define the word "religion" as we attempt to apply it to wider bodies of human action and belief.

The *study* of religion begins and ends with the idea that we are investigating the nature of the subject and hence are not wholly knowledgeable about it. Nonetheless we begin with certain assumptions, which suggest that we have a sufficient definition of our subject to determine at least what data are relevant to our study. Let us clarify those assumptions at the outset, because they will greatly shape our approach.

We will consider as religious those images, actions, and symbols that both express and define the extent and character of the world, especially those that provide the cosmic framework in which human life finds meaning and the terms of its fulfillment. We will also consider as religious those actions, processes, and symbols through which life is lived in order that it may be meaningful and purposive. But while we are referring to the grandest level of human action, conception, and imagination, let us not, at the same time, restrict where in the cultures we will look for relevant data. For Native American cultures, we will find aspects of religion in stories of creation, of heroes, of tricksters, of fools. We will find them in architecture, art, and orientations in the landscape. We will find them in ritual drama, costumes, masks, and ceremonial paraphernalia. We will find them related to hunting, farming, and fishing. We will find grand cosmological schemes and religious ideas in the rudest, most common materials and circumstances as well as in highly developed poetic, intellectual, and artistic forms.

The presentation of Native American religions usually entails organizing the massive quantities of data either by geographic area or type of phenomena. While the data are essential to the understanding of Native American religions, I do not consider the presentation of facts as the primary task of an introductory study. The facts are meaningful to us only in terms of the questions we ask of them. Thus I believe that for our limited purposes, we should organize our study directly around our questions. While I will present abundant data in the process of considering these questions, it is not my primary intention to give either a complete or orderly presentation of facts.

In the first three chapters, we will consider a series of questions that will illuminate basic aspects and attributes of Native American cultures—characteristics that shape religious thought and expression. These chapters will investigate fundamentals, the building blocks that constitute Native American religions and the tools that forge them. In Chapter 1, we will look into the processes involved in the formulation and expression of cosmologies, views of the shapes and processes of reality. We will ask what forms these take, what symbolic languages are utilized in their expression. We will inspect the general characteristics and attributes of these symbolic languages and inquire how they are creatively applied and utilized. In Chapter 2, we will focus on nonliteracy and ask to what extent orality shapes the character of Native American religions, particularly in terms of the roles of thought and speech. Chapter 3 will consider the character of symbols engaged in action; that is, when they are brought into action through ritual, speech, and visual forms. In this context, we will consider the character of ritual drama and ask what it does, how it functions, how it is creative, and how its many constituents contribute to the significance of the symbolic process.

In the next three chapters, we will turn to different kinds of questions that focus on types of religious phenomena commonly found in Native American cultures. Chapter 4 will inquire about the nature of religious forms and practices that correspond with the transitional moments in the individual cycle of life. In Chapter 5, we will consider the significance of the interrelationship between sustenance activities, by which cultures obtain their food, and religious actions and patterns. We will investigate situations in cultures that practice a variety of sustenance modes—hunting, gathering, and farming. Chapter 6 will turn to a consideration of the historical processes engaged by Native Americans in maintaining and developing their religious traditions. In this context, we will consider new and emergent forms of religion and ask what roles they play in the character of Native American religions.

We will use specific cultural examples for discussion and illustration throughout. I will present these in as full a manner as possible, though it will not often be possible to present the examples in their extended historical contexts. In this omission, I do not wish to fall prey to the interpretation that would suggest the image of the changeless or timeless "Indian." Chapter 6 will be devoted to the correction of this shortcoming.

We are at this point, of course, still in the boat with Columbus; and when we are through, we will probably believe that we have found some of the answers to our questions. Perhaps the advice that can best hold a rein on our errors is to remember that our very modest task is that of charting maps of the territory we circumscribe by the term "Native American religions"—and to recall, as Jonathan Z. Smith has so aptly phrased it, that "map is not territory."[14]

NOTES

1. The information on this story of Columbus is presented in Edmundo O'Gorman, *The Invention of America: An Inquiry into the Historical Nature of the New World and the Meaning of Its History* (Bloomington: Indiana University Press, 1961), especially pp. 71–125.
2. Ibid., p. 138.
3. Robert F. Berkhofer, Jr., *The White Man's Indian: Images of the American Indian from Columbus to the Present* (New York: Knopf, 1978), p. 3.
4. It is notable that Berkhofer adopts the term "Native American" to refer to the people, confining the term "Indian" to the European stereotypical image of the people. He does this because he says that "Indian" is a white invention and not a term the people used to refer to themselves. Yet on these grounds, surely "Native American" is also a white invention and should be equally inappropriate. It seems to me that what Berkhofer misses is that the term "Indian" is not an invention at all; and it is precisely because "Native American" *is* an invention that it is valuable.

5. The heading as well as much of the material presented in this section is drawn from Lewis Hanke, *All Mankind Is One: A Study of the Disputation between Bartolomé de Las Casas and Juan Gines de Sepúlveda in 1550 on the Intellectual and Religious Capacity of the American Indians* (DeKalb: Northern Illinois University Press, 1974).

6. Ibid., p. 9.

7. For a discussion of how the "we/they" relationship is fundamental to the nature of comparison—and how it has been reflected in various attitudes and scholarly styles in the history of the comparative study of cultures—see Jonathan Z. Smith, "*Adde Parvum Parvo Magnus Acervus Erit,*" *History of Religions* 11 (1971): 67–90.

8. Hanke, *All Mankind Is One*, p. 57 quoting the use of Acts 17:26 by Las Casas.

9. See also Berkhofer, *The White Man's Indian*, pp. 23–25.

10. See also Ibid., p. 26.

11. Ibid., p. 6.

12. Ibid., p. 8.

13. The only exception to this general avoidance that I know is the book by Catherine Albanese, *America: Religions and Religion* (Belmont, Ca: Wadsworth, 1981) that devotes a chapter to Native American religions.

14. Jonathan Z. Smith, *Map Is Not Territory* (Leiden: E. J. Brill, 1979), especially the essay "Map Is Not Territory," pp. 289–310.

CHAPTER 1

The Place to Begin

There are a large number of Native American peoples in North America. Each tribe is distinct, with its own language, its own history, its own religious institutions, traditions, practices, and beliefs. This diversity and complexity makes it difficult to find a starting point for considering Native American religions. If we choose the terminology and categories of any one tradition or those of Western religious traditions as the base from which to begin, we will likely prejudice all of the others. Still, we need some common question or set of questions to provide us with a beginning. We need some way to let the terms of each religious tradition speak as much as possible for themselves.

One place to begin is "in the beginning"; that is, with the stories and oral traditions that describe the world creation or the formation of tradition and culture. A neutral question to ask of these beginnings is what is the character of the reality established in these beginnings? What is the shape and what are the categories fundamental to this created world? Religion is expressed and practiced through these most basic categories of reality and world view. We will examine a number of examples in this chapter to illustrate this contention.

First we will consider several examples showing the diversity of ways in which religious principles, beliefs, and practices are reflected in the character given to the world by the shape it takes at creation.

RELIGION AND THE SHAPE OF THE WORLD

Zuni: The Middle Place

In 1528, the Spaniard Cabeza de Vaca survived shipwreck near American shores and wandered over what is now northern Mexico and parts of Texas until 1536, when he was rescued. He recounted stories told to him by "Indians" about the existence of seven golden cities at a place called Cibola. When this news reached Spain, an expedition was immediately commissioned to seek these golden cities. It was led by Fray Marcos de Niza, who took with him Estéban, the negro slave of Cabeza de Vaca. In May of 1539, this expedition succeeded in forcefully claiming one of seven Zuni villages, Hawikuh, for the King of Spain, but in the conquest Estéban was killed by the Zuni. Marcos de Niza reported having seen from a distance another village. The following year, Coronado found and captured the same village and named it Granada; continuing his conquest of the area, he found a total of seven Zuni villages. The golden color of the sunlit adobe did not impress the Spaniards, and Coronado continued to look for the seven cities of gold. This famed first contact with Native Americans in the territory now known as the United States, occurring more than 80 years before the *Mayflower* sailed, is important for more than historical fact.

While the Spanish did not recognize them as golden cities, the seven cities from the Zuni perspective bore meaning of cosmic significance that was obvious to them, yet completely beyond the grasp of the Spaniards. For the Zuni, their villages were not only of a golden hue; they embodied meanings fully as precious, in their number and location, as the Spanish value of gold.

According to Zuni stories of origin, in the beginning there existed only Awonawilona, an androgynous creator figure, who is conceived as something of a composite of all superhuman beings and is identified with the great vault of the heaven. All was fog rising like steam when Awonawilona breathed from his/her heart and created the clouds and waters. With the assistance of other creators, Awonawilona created the universe as it is known to the Zuni. In that first time, "when the earth was soft," the ancestors of the Zuni lived below the earth surface, in the dark and very crowded caves of the earth's womb. The Sun Father created two sons, war gods. Equipped with rainbows and lightning arrows for transportation, these two descended into the fourth world below the earth surface to bring the Zuni people out to the light of the sun. In Zuni, the word for life, *tekohananee*, literally means daylight; and the inner stuff of life, *tse'makwin*, literally means thoughts and is associated with the head, the heart, and the breath.[1] Upon emergence, the Zuni remained near the emergence place where, at intervals of four years, the earth would rumble and other peoples—the Hopi, the Navajo, the Mexicans—emerged from the lower worlds. They were the younger brothers and sisters to the Zuni.[2]

The instructions given the Zuni people were to embark upon a journey in search of the "middle place of the world." For many years the Zuni people traveled here and there, searching for this middle place. As they traveled in distinct groups, the deities instructed them to take names to identify themselves. This was the origin of Zuni clans and clan affiliations. Each time the Zuni settled, some disaster destroyed their village and forced them to move on, showing them that they had not yet ended their quest for the "middle place." Finally the Zuni came upon an old man who was a rain priest and who possessed a very sacred object. Their own rain priest prayed with this man, and together they caused much rain to fall. This signaled to the people that they had found the "middle place," and their anxiety was further allayed when a water strider came along, spread out its legs, and declared that the middle of the world would be directly beneath its heart. The Zuni villages were built here; one at the place beneath the heart, and one at each place marked by the six feet of the water strider. The esoteric or ceremonial name for the village of Zuni is *Itiwana*, which means "the middle." Enshrined at the most central spot were the sacred objects of the rain priests, and this marks the exact middle of the world. The Zuni conceive of their world as a large island of earth completely surrounded by oceans. Lakes and springs on the island open to an underground water system that interconnects the oceans.

The seven Zuni villages that Coronado found were perhaps constructed upon this archetype. These villages did not survive the Spanish conquest. The present village of Zuni was founded in 1683 and has remained the only Zuni village except for the villages occupied during agricultural seasons near Zuni farms. It was not until the mid-19th century that ethnographers began to learn that a seven-part cosmological structure existed in the minds of the Zuni people and that this formed the basic division in the village and social organization of the Zuni. The Zuni consider that their village reflects the very structure of the cosmos, the basic shape of which is described as an orientation around seven points—the four cardinal directions, the zenith (above), the nadir (below), and the center. It is notable that in the present village of Zuni, however, this correspondence is ideological and not physical, since the village is not neatly layed out with seven distinct physical quarters. Let us review the general dimensions of this cosmological order as it is held by the Zuni.

The sevenfold pattern is a system of orientation within time and space, defined in such a way that each place is meaningfully distinguished from and related to all other places. The emphasis is as much on defining interrelationships as upon making distinctions. The Zuni people are given distinct roles that are complexly interrelated in the terms of place within this sevenfold scheme. Zuni clans are organized into seven groups. Each group, especially those that correspond with the cardinal directions, has distinctions and social roles described in the temporal and spatial terms associated with its place. For example, the Crane, Grouse, and Evergreen-oak clans are placed in the north, which is associated with winter and with yellow, the color of morning and evening light in the winter as well as the color of the northern auroral lights. The clan symbols are appropriate to the place and its attributes: The crane's flight announces coming winter, the grouse changes its color to white in winter, and the evergreen-oak stays as green in winter as other trees do in summer. This domain has associations with wind, air, and breath as well as with activities that center on war and destruction. The other cardinal directions follow this pattern of associations.[3]

We can begin to see that the whole system embodies a totality that is identical to the life process. As the annual cycle of life unfolds through the sequence of seasons, the various directions, and their peoples and attributes, each in turn comes to play the central and dominant role. Each is meaningless except as it contributes to the whole.

With this simplest of introductions to a system that is actually multileveled and much more complex, we can consider the significance of the middle place. We can approach this in at least two ways: The middle place is (1) one of the seven places distinct from, yet related to, the other six places; but (2), it is also a summation, composite, or symbol of the totality. It is the one point common to all other domains, to all other distinct places. It is the place where all the others interrelate and interact as a totality. This middle place is identified with the heart, the seat of life, the most sacred life-giving objects. Consequently the middle place is at once the enshrined sacred object, the village (whose

name means the middle place), and the cosmos when seen as a whole.
Even the creator deity has this ambivalent character of being both a
distinct deity and a composite of all other deities. In the terms of the
Zuni origin and migration stories, the middle place is that place where
life is possible, as opposed to those places that are intolerable or where
life cannot exist.

This brings to mind the scene in Carlos Castaneda's book *The Teachings of Don Juan*, in which Carlos was given the task of finding his own
place on don Juan's porch. He thought this a ridiculous task but
undertook it. After trying many positions, he finally began to perceive
great discomfort associated with various places on the porch, so un-
comfortable or frightening that he had to move from them. He continued moving from place to place in this manner until, exhausted, he
fell asleep on the porch. When don Juan came out the next morning, he
awakened Carlos and said, "Oh, I see you have found your place."[4]

We can understand the Zuni notion of *itiwana* or middle place better
if we consider the Zuni calendar. It is divided into two parts by the
solstices, and each part is further divided into six lunar months. The
months for each half of the year bear the same names; hence both
December and June, the months of the solstices, are called *I'kopu*,
which means "turning and looking back," referring to the action of the
sun reaching its farthermost point and turning back. During these
winter and summer solstice months, there is a 20-day period designated as *itiwana*. These middle places in the year are significant times
for the celebration and ceremonial creation of a new phase of the year.
The making of a new time has the designation of middle place because
it denotes the coming together of all the ceremonial societies that
perform in turn during the remainder of the year. It is the grasping of
the totality, an act of integration, which gives it the significance of
middle place. In a sense, this period *itiwana* is a period that embodies
all of time in strong, highly symbolic form; seen in this way, such
periods are clearly of very great significance to the Zuni people. They
consider that life itself depends upon and proceeds from these middle
places in time.

Even with this simplified presentation of the Zuni world view, we
can appreciate the rich complexity of the symbol system by which the
Zuni place themselves in a way that integrates individual life, clan life,
village life, and history (both ordinary and sacred). These human
affairs are identified with the very character of the world. We can also
understand why, for the Zuni, the worth of human life is defined by

and evaluated in terms of orientations in time and space, as described by this complex system. The village is ideologically, if not physically, a cosmic and religious symbol.

Reflecting back on the Spanish quest for the seven golden cities, we can now compare perspectives. For the Spanish, the worth of a person was measured in the amount of gold possessed; but for the Zuni, it was measured in terms of the character of the place on which a person stands.[5]

It seems clear that if we should attempt to understand anything of Zuni religion (or any other Native American religion, as we will show) without placing it in the context of this broad framework of the cosmology and religious world view, we would severely limit our degree of understanding from their perspective. The neutral question—the question that gives us a place to begin—concerns the shape of reality, the way in which the world is viewed and valued. This is a question that begins with simple terms of time and space; but it ends by giving us entrance to a way of trying to see the world as others see it. It gives us a place from which to try mapping their world and religion as they see and know it.

We have seen that the center is important for the Zuni; but as we are about to see, it is not always a matter of finding the center.

Seneca: The Creator Twins

It is common in many Native American cultures to account for the nature of the world by telling stories of twin brothers whose actions created the world in primal times. One brother is the principal creator who attempts to create a world that is perfect, a utopia for human beings; but he is followed by his brother, who undoes and reverses much of the creator brother's work. Consequently, since the world is the result of the work of both brothers, the brother must also be seen as a creator figure. This type of story is known among tribes all over North America. The version of the Seneca follows this pattern:

> In the beginning before there was an earth, there was a world in the sky. In that place, everything was filled with life that radiated from a giant tree standing in the center of that world. It emitted light half the time and was dark half the time, thus making day and night for the people. Everything there was perfect. There was no want for food. Death did not exist. One family had five sons, and the youngest fell in love with a girl. Feelings of love made this youth weak, for he longed to marry the girl. They were married, but he continued to grow weaker. In a dream, he was told that his brothers should pull up the tree of life by its roots, lest he die. The tree was

to provide for the creation of a new world below, and a young tree would grow to replace it in this sky world. The brothers did as instructed, and the tree fell inward into the world below through the hole it had left in the sky. The youth took his wife to the rim of the hole and while they were sitting there, the wind from below blew on the woman and impregnated her. The youth knew that his wife was to be mother to the new world below, so he pushed her off the rim.

Her fall into this new world was eventually broken by a flock of birds that carried her until they could find support for her, since the world was only water. Only the big turtle was strong enough to hold her, and he became the support for the new world. All of the animals dived into the water to seek earth with which to make the world.[6]

When the earth was greatly expanded to its present size, the woman gave birth to a daughter. The daughter approached womanhood, and her mother forbade her to play in the water. But the daughter did so, and the water impregnated her with twins. Even in their mother's womb, the twins began to fight with one another. When it was time for them to be born, one brother was born in the normal way, but the other was too eager and burst a hole in his mother's side, thus killing her. The grandmother buried her daughter, and from her body grew corn and other food plants for the future human beings. She gave the names of *Tarachiawagon*, Good Spirit, and *Tawiskaron*, Bad Spirit, to the boys.

When the twins grew to manhood, they set out on their tasks. The Good Spirit made the form of human beings, male and female, in the dust and breathed life into them. He created the good and useful plants and animals of the world. He created the rivers and lakes. He even made the current run both ways in the streams to make travel easy. Meanwhile, the Bad Spirit busied himself with the creation of annoying and monstrous animals, pests, plant blight, and diseases for human beings. He introduced death. He turned the currents in the streams so they would only run one way. Once he even stole the sun. The Good Spirit tried to reverse these things, but he was not able to reverse them all.

Finally the twin brothers met at the west rim of the world. The Bad Spirit was at this time in the form of a giant. They decided to have a contest to determine which was the stronger and thus settle their struggles once and for all. Their chosen task was the feat of moving the Rocky Mountains. The Bad Spirit tried first and was able to move them, but only a little. When it came time for the Good Spirit to try, he asked his brother to turn his back to the mountains; then he moved the mountains right against this brother's back. When the Good Spirit told him he could turn around and look, the Bad Spirit bashed his nose against the mountain, and a crooked nose has characterized his appearance ever since.

The Bad Spirit pleaded with his brother not to kill him. His wish was granted, but only on the condition that he would serve henceforth to help take care of human beings. Consequently the Seneca and other Iroquoian peoples have societies that prepare masks used to impersonate the many forms of this bad brother; but their ritual acts are aimed at the cure of disease and the dispersion of witchcraft and other destructive agents.[7]

This story is complex and carries many themes deserving discussion. For our immediate concerns, however, we can notice a marked difference from the Zuni understanding of the character of the world and its creation. Certainly along with the Zuni, the Seneca (on the basis of this story) highly value those actions that conform to expectations. The brother who is born the "proper" way is the "good" brother. The brother who destroys his mother by bursting through her side in the "improper" way is a destroyer. The actions of the brothers distinguish their evaluation as good or bad, while at the same time they set the model for good and bad acts in human culture. But we find the Seneca cosmology introducing the idea that while such violations are bad, they nonetheless contribute to the shape and way of the world, as evidenced by the existence of pests, disease, death, and witchcraft. Instead of the Zuni search for that middle place where life forces are so delicately balanced that life-negating forces are nullified, the Seneca embrace those life-negating forces, institutionalizing them in the Society of Faces (whose members wear the masks manifesting the Bad Spirit)—but for the effect of turning them, as in a mirror, back upon themselves. The Society of Faces performs all sorts of acts on the model of the Bad Spirit, but they do so in order to cure disease, fight witchcraft, and remove disorder. Comprehending the Seneca perspective on the power of the Faces without placing them in the framework of the Seneca cosmology and religious world view would be most difficult.

Navajo: The Suffering Hero

Most Navajo stories tell of the heroes who lived in the sacred era after the world was created but before it was inhabited by the Navajo people. Many of these stories center on the adventures of the heroes, the consequences of their failures, and their resulting travail and misfortunes. Navajos feel that all the stories of heroes stem from the stories of the creation of the world, so we too must at least briefly acquaint ourselves with these creation stories before looking at an example of a story of a Navajo hero.

Like their Zuni neighbors, the Navajo trace their origins from far beneath the present earth surface. They tell of four and sometimes more worlds stacked one on top of another below this earth-surface world. In these lower worlds at a time before the Navajo world was created lived insect and animal peoples, who acted in a manner resembling the Navajo. The stories set in these lower worlds tell of strife, disorder, and confusion. No matter how hard these peoples tried, they could not stop fighting and committing wrongful acts like incest and adultery. As a result of their actions, each of the worlds on which they attempted to live was destroyed, and they were forced to find new places to live. As their forced journey of emergence progressed, the need became more and more urgent for a world in which all living things would know their proper places and live according to rules so that order would exist. Still the forces of disorder persisted, and such things as witchcraft, disease, and all sorts of strife were introduced. The landscape of these lower worlds bore the barren character of the life patterns followed there.

Finally having caused the destruction of the worlds in which they lived, the peoples emerged onto the present earth surface, which was free of features because it was covered with water. With spiritual help, they succeeded in getting the water drained and the muds dried; and those who had emerged planned how they would give form to this new world. This was accomplished through ritual acts, performed first in a sweat lodge and then in a hogan (the name for the ordinary Navajo home, which is also used as a ceremonial place). Pieces of jewel from the medicine bundle of First Man were laid upon the floor, forming a painting to represent the various things that were to exist in the world. Features of the earth were shown, as well as its plant and animal life. Then in a magical act of prayer, song, and breath, this symbolic representation of the world was transformed into the world to become *dinetáh* or Navajoland. The creation hogan was itself a living form whose support pillars were the holy people who hold up the sky. Though a hogan appears rude in form and construction, its dome shape and earthen floor bear the structure of the cosmos.

The principle of order followed in these acts of creation was one of creating complementary pairs and placing them across from each other so that they balance on the rim of the emergence place. The world, for example, is bounded by four sacred mountains, which are perceived as deities. These mountains stand at the four corners of the world at the cardinal directions and have associated attributes similar to those described for the Zuni. The east mountain and deity stand across from the west, complementing one another.

The result of the creation of the earth surface was a world in which everything was in order and placed properly so that its forces were delicately balanced against all other forces on the center point. The deities that are the life forms of dawn and evening twilight were sent on a tour of all the mountains to inspect the creation; and as they proceeded from one vantage point to another, they found everything in place, which is the very definition, in Navajo terms, of beauty (*hózhó*).

It is this world that Navajo heroes enter, a world in which everything exists in its proper place and with everything delicately balanced on a fulcrum at the center of the world, the emergence place. As we will see, the heroism of these figures lies in the courage that enabled them to meet the requirement of living and moving about in this world so delicately balanced—for the very living of life leads to a disturbance of this world of beauty and threatens its collapse into chaos.[8] This cosmic drama is reflected in the adventures and plight of the hero. Let us consider one brief adventure of a Navajo heroic figure:

> A young man traveling with his family departed by himself for a hunting trip to supply them with food. During his trip, he met a beautiful young woman, and they visited with each other. He became fond of her and spent the night, during which they had sexual contact. She neglected to tell him until later that she was the wife of White Thunder. The next morning, the youth continued his hunt and eventually killed a mountain sheep. He observed that its left horn bore the mark of zigzag lightning, and its left eye was missing. He ignored this omen of the wrath of White Thunder and butchered the animal, preparing to take the meat back to his family. But the sky clouded over, and it began to rain. The hunter took refuge under a spruce tree, keeping his arrows with him for protection. While he waited there, lightning struck the ground all around him. Each time, he heard a voice in the sky say, "He has not yet been struck. He does not lay his arrows aside!" The hunter wondered at this and, curious to see what would happen, he set his arrows against the tree. White Thunder was then able to get past the hunter's magical protection and in an instant struck the hunter with lightning, shattering him beyond recognition. Nothing was left of him but a streak of blood.
>
> When the hunter failed to return, his family went in search of him. They found out what had happened and were told that only Gila Monster could help them. When they contacted Gila Monster, he demonstrated his powers of restoration by cutting himself up and scattering his various parts broadly about. These parts were gathered together, reassembled, and restored to life, all according to his powers and knowledge. Gila Monster then restored the hunter to life in a ceremonial that used this same knowledge and power. The ritual of restoration served not only to restore life to the hunter, but initiated him into the knowledge and powers of Gila Monster. This heroic adventure then gave origin to the Navajo tradition of ceremonial restoration known as Flintway, one of the ways by which Navajos bring order to a situation threatened by chaos, death, and disease.[9]

This story follows a typical scenario for Navajo hero stories. The heroes, invariably in the process of a journey, enter forbidden territories or violate some regulation that is often unknown to them. As a consequence, they suffer in any number of ways, even to almost complete annihilation. When the heroes are unable to get out of their predicaments, mythological figures with special powers come to aid and relieve their suffering by performing ceremonials that restore them and also initiate the heroes into knowledge of the ceremonial ways.

Whereas the Navajo eras of creation were principally concerned with establishing proper places and relationships for things in the world, the era of these heroes is concerned more with how one lives in the world. It deals with the boundaries of both places and relationships, with the relationships necessary for life, such as those between hunter and game, between husband and wife (and women not his wife), between in-laws, between the living and the dead, between Navajos and non-Navajos, between a person and the plants and animals in the environment, between human beings and deities. The effect of these stories is to define the Navajo way of life by testing limits and by reinforcing those limits through the adventures of the suffering heroes. By considering extensive ceremonial systems, which comprise much of Navajo ritual, we can better understand how they serve to reconstitute the balanced conditions of creation that may be disrupted as part of the very process of living.

Conclusion

Through these initial examples, it should be clear that any effort to understand the religion of any Native American people must include some consideration of their view of the world. We must attempt to understand their religion in the terms by which the people themselves understand the character of reality. These terms are defined, given distinction and form, in the dimensions of time and space. Even the unseen aspects of reality are given symbolic expression through these concrete terms.

One way of acquiring these basic terms and understanding something of their religious significance is by considering the stories of the creation of the world or of the major transformations that gave the world its present shape. It is not only the nature of Native Americans, but of religious humanity generally, to conceive and express the nature of the world in the temporal and spatial terms of place. Indeed it is, as we have seen, the symbolic language of place that gives orientation to social, cultural, and religious forms and expresses the meaning of life and its destiny. We must learn to see beyond our own initial confusion and disbelief in what may appear as the fanciful character of Native

American stories; for they hold the symbolic language bearing the perspective and world views distinct to each culture.

Other aspects of this most fundamental concern can be illuminated by observing that our three examples have certain similarities but also major distinctions. We can appreciate the fact that it is no simple exercise to state or understand this symbolic language of place for even one Native American culture. We can also see that for all three cultures in our examples, the character of place takes shape in terms of how the culture is able to resolve the conflicting needs for a clearly defined sense of place—that is, rules and boundaries that define all human actions—and for unbounded freedom unfettered by rules or boundaries. In all three cases, the character of well-defined rules and boundaries is established not by dogmatism, but by permitting infringement upon proper place. This violation or infringement is also not confined to some story set in the primordial era of heroes; it has been incorporated into the very structure of religious practices and ceremonial performances. We must understand that, quite contrary to the way they are often romantically and simplistically presented, Native American views of reality are not static structures in which reality is divided, for example, into four mystical parts divided by the cardinal coordinates; but tend to incorporate the many dynamic and conflicting elements that are inseparable from the nature of human life—life and death, the constriction of rules and the insecurity of having no rules, good and evil, change and continuity. Further, Native Americans embody the struggle with the nature of human existence both in the content and form of their stories and through their rituals and ordinary life ways.

THE TRICKSTER

The human desire to be free of rules, to be unbound by time, space, or society, is dramatically and often humorously played out in many Native American cultures in the stories of what we call the trickster. The figure we refer to by that term is really unnamable and undefinable except by saying that his character is free of any of those restricting elements that give something definition and thus a name. To be distinguishable means that a figure must have some particular characteristics, ways, or appearances; but for this figure, the only dependable characteristic is that he defies definition. In many Native American cultures, this figure takes the form of a coyote, but a very unusual coyote. In some cultures, he has no particular form and can transform himself into any number of appearances. He is, in any case, the subject of numerous stories told throughout native North America, and we must consider this figure in terms of our concern with the symbolic language of place. Most notably, these stories are told much more often than stories of the creation of the world and are told particularly to children. They doubtless serve extensively to introduce and define elements of the world view to members of the culture.

The flavor of trickster stories is shown in the well-known story of Eye-juggler. The Cheyenne version goes like this:

> There was a man who could send his eyes out of his head to a limb of a tree, and they would come back when called. Trickster ("White Man" is the Cheyenne name) wanted to do this, and he learned how from the man. But he was warned that he could do it no more than four times in one day. Trickster liked to do this because of the vantage he gained, but he paid no attention to the warning. One day when he sent his eyes out for the fifth time, he sent them to the highest tree he could find; but when he called them to return, they didn't. He called and waited and called and waited, but they didn't come back. Flies gathered on them as they started to spoil.
>
> Trickster lay on the ground unable to see and waited for something to happen. Soon a mouse approached and crawled on Trickster to snip a piece of hair for its nest. Trickster was thus able to catch it and force it to lead him around. The mouse pleaded to be released but wasn't let go until it gave Trickster one of its eyes. Trickster could then see, but the mouse's eye was so small that it went far back into Trickster's eye socket.
>
> Trickster then saw a buffalo grazing nearby. He told the buffalo his trouble and began to cry. The buffalo pitied him and gave him one of its eyes, but it was so large that it wouldn't go into Trickster's eye socket.[10]

This story is told many ways and can be made to apply to innumerable specific incidents, but the general lesson is clear. When Trickster ignores the restrictions placed on him, he suffers in consequence.

In other stories of Trickster, it is his sexual urges that remain unbounded. The Winnebago tell a story of a trickster who had such a long penis that he had to carry it coiled up in a box on his back:

> One day he went down to a lake and saw a number of girls swimming on the opposite shore. Attempting to use the advantage of his long penis, he dispatched it across the lake, but it tended to float. After several attempts at weighting it with rocks so it would go at the proper depth, he successfully lodged it in the chief's daughter. Various people were called to try to help the girl get free of this thing, but they didn't know what it was and couldn't help her. Finally an old woman was found who knew the ways of Trickster. She stood astride Trickster's penis and gouged it with an awl. Trickster pulled his penis back so quickly that the old woman was thrown a great distance.[11]

A plains version of this story places Trickster across a prairie from the women. The resolution comes when a herd of buffalo stampede between Trickster and the women, cutting his penis to its present size. The trod-upon pieces were then transformed into the animals of the prairie.

The utopian urges expressed in Trickster—that is, his urges to be unbound and without limitations—often deal with food, for his appetite is insatiable and he never works for what he eats. We see this in a Menomini story of a trickster:

> Two blind men were moved across the lake from the rest of the people where they might be safer. They were provided with food, and a rope was stretched from their lodge to the lake so they could find their way to the water. Racoon came by one day and watched what was going on. Each day one blind man would cook while the other went for water, and the next day they would trade jobs. Their food looked good to Racoon, so he played a trick on them in order to get some. When it was time to eat, one blind man started to cook the meat while the other went for water, but Racoon had moved the rope from the lake and tied it to a bush. The blind man who went for water returned distressed by the fact that the lake had dried up and that they would die without water. Racoon then replaced the rope, and when the other blind man went to try finding water, he found the lake and got water. While this was taking place, Racoon placed himself in the lodge and waited for the meat to be cooked. Eight pieces were prepared and placed between the two blind men. Racoon took four and started eating them while he watched what happened. Each of the blind men began to accuse the other of taking more than his share, and when their tempers were at a high pitch, Racoon slapped them both in the face, thus making each think that the other had done it. While they rolled about fighting, Racoon took the rest of the food and laughed out loud as he left. The men stopped fighting when they realized what had happened, and Racoon told them they should learn not to find fault with each other so easily.[12]

An Apache version of this story concerns Coyote and two blind women. It ends in Coyote's inflicting a cruel death upon the two women.[13]

Trickster is an important figure in the oral traditions of many Native American peoples, and from these several stories we can perhaps see why. In Trickster is embodied the human struggle against the confinement felt by being bound to place, even within the obvious necessity of such definition in order to prevent chaos. In many of his adventures, Trickster permits people to experience the vicarious thrills and freedoms of a utopian existence. But his folly reveals the very meaning of the boundaries that give order to human life. It is certainly clear that, to Native American people, these stories have far more significance than "simple entertainment," the status consigned to them by most interpretive studies.

STRUCTURES OF REALITY IN ARCHITECTURE AND ART

As previously mentioned, the symbolic language of place—the set of symbols that gives the people of a culture orientation in space and time—is pervasive in Native American cultures. While we may see this most easily in the language of stories, it exists as well in many other symbolic forms. Native American cultures have been especially consistent in their use of this symbolic language throughout the many forms that give distinction to a culture. As we have already seen in the examples cited, this symbolic language of place is found in social structure, in mythic geography, and in architecture. The village of Zuni replicates the cosmic pattern, as do the Navajo hogan and ancestral lands. We find in many Native American cultures that landscapes, villages, ceremonial grounds, ceremonial lodges, and common homes replicate the form and process of the cosmos. This has been commonly recognized, but a tendency has existed to reduce the many, widely varying examples to the oversimplistic and all-inclusive model of the sacred circle. This is not accurate.

We can appreciate the complexity of the cosmic symbolism that can be borne by architectural forms in a brief examination of the symbolism in the Delaware/Lenape Big House. The term "Big House" refers both to a ceremony and the structure in which it takes place. From the Delaware/Lenape point of view, the religion of the Big House stems from the origin of the world, and they feel that all other religions have emerged from it. We shall see why.

The lodge is built with four walls covered by a partial roof open in the center, through which extends the center pole erected in the lodge floor. The lodge bears simple cosmic symbolism in its equation of the floor with the earth, the walls with the four quarters of the world, and the roof with the vault of the sky. On the center post is carved the face image of *mesi'ŋgok*, the creator and supreme power. The lodge centers on this figure, as does the religion. The pole rooted in the earth pierces the sky through the 12 levels that form the abode of *mesi'ŋgok*. He holds the top of the pole in his hand. Faces carved on the support pillars on each wall represent the *manitou* or spirits of these cosmic regions.

The lodge has doors on the east and west that are associated, respectively, with the rising sun, a symbol of the beginning of things, and the setting sun, a symbol of the end of things. Beneath the earthen floor are the underworlds.

The order of movement in the lodge is to enter by the east door, moving in a circular direction to the north around the center pole, and exiting by the west door. This movement is identified as the "white path," which symbolizes the cycle of life. Within the lodge are specified places for people in the three clan groupings—wolf, turtle, and turkey—and for the men who sit apart from the women.

The Big House ceremony symbolizes transit through the year. It transpires over 12 nights, symbolizing the 12 moons or lunar months of the year. The dancing that follows the "white path" symbolizes the east-to-west movement of the sun as well as the passage of life from birth to death.

This is but the most simple description of the symbolic language of place borne in the Big House religion of the Delaware/Lenape. It is carried out in much greater detail and throughout the many smaller elements of the costuming, face painting, ritual paraphernalia, and ritual procedures. [14]

Throughout native North America, cosmic symbolism is also introduced through the artwork that is so intricate a part of clothing, utensils, masks, drums, and ritual objects. The well-known sacred pipe of the Sioux and other peoples bears the symbols of the plants, animals, birds, various domains of the universe, seasons, and history of the people, all of which are brought together with the spiritual world in the prayerful act of smoking the pipe. [15]

Through the processes of craftsmanship, we can glimpse the aesthetic vision of the world held by Native Americans. The old tradition of Eskimo carving, before the existence of a tourist and curio market, was a process in which the carver (and all Eskimo men were carvers) saw and revealed the form that lay within the uncarved materials. The carver would hold the unworked piece of ivory, turning it in his hands, contemplating it until he could see what form was hidden within it. Carving was not a process of the artist conquering or commanding the raw materials to conform to his ideas. It was rather a process of releasing the form already resident in the material. [16]

We see this again in a dialogue between two contemporary Pacific Northwest Coast craftsmen, Bill Holm and Bill Reid, as they consider some old pipes. Reid speaks of the wood-carving process as being driven by a "crazy mystique of the object inside the wood." Holm

Prayerful act of offering the pipe

agrees with this, saying, "The artist has to see that form in there." And Reid then says that the craftsman must have "the courage to take it [the carving] beyond the point your mind tells you is logical."[17] From this we can see that the view of reality, that sense of the shape of things, is not only in the visual objects; it is also a part of the very process by which these objects are created. The process is not one of dogmatically applying form or structure to raw material or of consciously creating symbols to stand for one's ideas. It is a process of seeing that the principles and forms of reality are already present in all things, even in an uncarved piece of ivory or wood, even in the most common, every-day things.

This brings us to the next level of this subject, as well as to one of my own favorite passages.

COSMICIZATION OF THE ORDINARY

Lame Deer was a wily old Oglala when he and his white friend Richard Erdoes engaged in composing his biography (published in 1972). He had lived his long life during the most difficult period in the history of the peoples of the northern plains, a period characterized by the constant threat of complete collapse and loss of cultural identity. This did not greatly embitter Lame Deer, although he liked to take advantage of aspects of his culture to point up its spiritual richness against what he felt was the impoverished spiritual condition of European-American culture.

One such example is very important for showing how the most common objects may reflect grand cosmic principles. It is a kind of meditation on a soot-covered cooking pot. Speaking to Erdoes, Lame Deer said:

> What do you see here, my friend? Just an ordinary old cooking pot, black with soot and full of dents.
>
> It is standing on the fire on top of that old wood stove, and the water bubbles and moves the lid as the white steam rises to the ceiling. Inside the pot is boiling water, chunks of meat with bone and fat, plenty of potatoes.
>
> It doesn't seem to have a message, that old pot, and I guess you don't give it a thought . . .
>
> But I'm an Indian. I think about ordinary, common things like this pot. The bubbling water comes from the rain cloud. It represents the sky. The fire comes from the sun which warms us all—men, animals, trees. The meat stands for the four-legged creatures, our animal brothers, who gave of themselves so that we should live. The steam is living breath. It was water; now it goes up to the sky, becomes a cloud again. These things are sacred. Looking at that pot full of good soup, I am thinking how, in this simple manner, Wakan Tanka takes care of me. We Sioux spend a lot of time thinking about everyday things, which in our mind are mixed up with the spiritual . . . We Indians live in a world of symbols and images where the spiritual and the commonplace are one . . . We try to understand them not with the head but with the heart, and we need no more than a hint to give us the meaning.[18]

It is common in Native American cultures to find iconic motifs; that is, meaningful visual patterns that appear in art, architecture, songs, prayers, stories, and ritual processes. I would like to trace one of these motifs related to the Navajo example presented earlier.

We saw in the discussion of the Navajo hero stories that a tension is maintained between a static, balanced order that characterizes the state of perfect beauty and the necessary disruption of that order and beauty as a part of the life process. The dynamic character of that tension is reflected in the iconic motif of the broken circle, which is ubiquitous in Navajo culture. Its most common incidence is as a circular enclosure with an opening or doorway, as in the Navajo hogan and sweat lodge. It appears in both the design and coil construction of Navajo baskets, in the incised design that encircles the neck of Navajo pottery jars, in the pathway or break in the border designs of Navajo weaving, and in the encircling guardian of a sandpainting. Movement within a hogan, especially during ceremonies, occurs in a pattern that prevents enclosed circles.

Navajo wedding basket

The broken circle nonetheless constitutes a boundary. It sets off a space and gives it significance. The break or opening that is the most distinctive aspect of the motif serves in a pragmatic sense as an orientation device. That position is the one to be aligned with the east or to define the direction east. It is the point to which all other points are related. But at another level, we find that the Navajo people consider the break or opening as a pathway leading out of the enclosed space. It is always seen as the "road out," and this road is the road of life. Navajos say that to draw a closed circle around someone's house would cause sickness, perhaps even death. It would be a symbolic obstruction of the life road going out.

Navajos have a funerary custom related to the meaning of this motif. If a person dies in a hogan, the body is not carried out the door, for carrying it along the road of life would be highly inappropriate. Consequently, the body is removed through a hole knocked in the north side of the hogan.

Recalling the stories of Navajo heroes, we can see that this iconic motif of the broken circle visually bears the concepts central to those stories. These concepts can be summarized as follows: The world was created in perfect beauty, but perfect beauty means a static order; since life is a dynamic process requiring movement, it risks destroying this beauty; so as disorder arises and life is threatened, one must be able to reconstitute order and beauty in the world; and this is done by ceremonial means, which recreate the pattern of perfect beauty.

The Navajo way of life is a process of moving from a domain of perfect beauty into history, only to return periodically upon the threat of chaos to achieve re-creation in the midst of that most sacred environment. Navajo life can be portrayed as a pathway out of the sacred domain into history, into the profane world. But it also provides a way in which even disorder and the threatening aspects of life may be seen as meaningful, real, and necessary. The pathway or break in the circle shows that the space inside and the space outside, the time of the gods in the beginning and the time of humans in history, the world of beauty and order and the world of ugliness and disorder, are intimately interdependent. It shows that the cosmic processes occur in the individual and that the sufferings of the individual are part of cosmic processes. The ubiquitous broken circle symbolizes this fundamental element in the Navajo world view.

CONCLUSION

This chapter has used selected examples to demonstrate that an essential task toward understanding any aspect of a Native American religion is to comprehend as fully as possible the culture's world view, that broadest framework which gives shape to the whole of reality. Through the examples presented, we have seen that we can often perceive this world view most immediately in stories, especially stories that tell of the creation of the world—for in the process of creation, the world is given its broadest order and shape. We have also seen that the language by which any culture expresses this framework is a symbolic language of place. Consequently anything in the material world, thus having the attributes of time and space, can bear these cosmic structures. Literally anything can be a symbol of the shape of reality or some aspect thereof.

The examples presented have also shown that no generally applicable Native American view of reality exists and that the many diverse views are complex and sophisticated. It is especially important for us to see that Native American views of reality are not at all static. Among the examples, we found none expressing the view that sacred things and religious significance can only occur in a rigidly defined place. Each world view bestows a certain creative power and therefore place, even to the very acts of the violation of order, within reality. Hence disease, death, trespass, witchcraft, and the like are all matters of great religious significance even though they are not given a positive moral value. The Seneca Bad Spirit, the trickster, the trespassing Navajo heroes are all essential for revealing and defining the true nature of reality. Consequently they are religious, meaningful figures. They embody the struggles and dynamics distinctive of human nature.

We can also see in the examples that, for Native Americans, reality itself is rooted in the spiritual world. The most basic and dependable level of reality is the spiritual level, the realm of deities, mythic heroes, and spirits. It is quite common in Native American cultures to perceive a spiritual character within every living thing, a spiritual entity that is the life force. And many things in the inanimate natural world are perceived as having life. Being itself derives from a manifestation of the spiritual world. The true nature of reality must be "seen" or found by human beings. A knowledge of reality must be won by revelations, by heroes, by folly; yet the knowledge is borne in the stories of these sacred events as well as in the many forms distinctive of the culture. An examination of Native American religious cultures tends to reveal that they find everything, down to the most common cooking pot, spiritually and cosmically relevant.

One final point is the image of the sacred circle, which is a frequent model used in presenting Native American views of reality. As a general view applicable to all Native American tribes, this model is simply erroneous. For many tribes, it is the square that is sacred—as for example, in the Creek and Natchez, whose ceremonial grounds were square, and in the square structures of the Delaware Big House and the Hopi kiva. But more significant is that even for cultures that do use circles in their symbolism, the presentation of the sacred circle image as a model is commonly most inadequate.

This image of the "Indian" sacred circle tends to amplify a highly romantic picture of peoples living in harmony and peace with each other and with nature. It is not a realistic view of human life for peoples whose entire histories have been filled with hardship, disease, death, discomfort, and difficulties. This mistaken view leads us to perceive Native Americans as static in their views of reality, as closed to change, and locked into changeless and timeless traditions. It leads us to identify the plight of all Native Americans with the pathetic image of Black Elk at the end of his life, when he lamented the broken state of the great hoop of the nations. We are led to feel with Black Elk that when the hoop is broken, the tradition has come to its end, and we lament this end with him. This is far from a correct characterization of all Native American world views.

The examples given have shown that Native American world views are especially dynamic in terms of their including, and even identifying as sacred, the disturbing, disruptive elements that are inseparable from life. They may hold an image of beauty and harmony, but it is a goal, while the path toward it is tempered with the hard facts of reality: that beauty and harmony are never fully achieved, except perhaps in death at an old age won by a long life of struggle. We have shown that Native American world views are not simply an eternal sacred cycle of reenacting the sacred events revealed by the deities in the world's beginning. They are open to history, to change, to threats from both within and outside the culture. If we could review the history of the last millennium of almost any tribe, we would find that it has undergone extensive changes, often amounting to physical movements of great distances, and major alterations in its way of life. Particularly in the last five centuries, which have brought increasing pressure on Native American peoples by the infringement of European-American cultures, Native American tribes have been forced to undergo incredible changes. The persistence and survival of so many of these tribes testify to the great capacity of Native American world views to accept and digest change while remaining in continuity with the defining elements of their traditions. This persistence has not been a product of isolation and extreme conservatism but of incorporating into their world views a flexibility that enables them to see patterns of the cosmic dramas even within the challenges of modernity. We will consider this development more extensively in Chapter 6.

1. Ruth L. Bunzel, *Introduction to Zuni Ceremonialism*, Smithsonian Institution, Bureau of American Ethnology, 47th Annual Report (Washington, D.C., 1929), p. 481.

2. See the following for the creation mythology of the Zuni: Ruth L. Bunzel, "Zuni Texts," *Publications of the American Ethnological Society* 15 (1933); Frank H. Cushing, *Outline of Zuni Creation Myths*, Smithsonian Institute, Bureau of American Ethnology, 13th Annual Report (Washington, D.C., 1896), pp. 325–447; E. C. Parsons, "The Origin Myth of Zuni," *Journal of American Folklore* 36 (1923): 135–62; and Dennis Tedlock, *Finding the Center: Narrative Poetry of the Zuni Indians* (New York: Dial, 1972).

3. Frank H. Cushing, *Outline of Zuni Creation Myths*, pp. 367–73.

4. Carlos Castaneda, *The Teachings of Don Juan* (New York: Ballantine, 1968), pp. 19–21.

5. For a discussion of the significance of this issue in the study of religion, see Jonathan Z. Smith, *Map Is Not Territory* (Leiden: E. J. Brill, 1979), especially the essays "The Influence of Symbols on Social Change: A Place on Which to Stand," pp. 129–46; and "Map Is Not Territory," pp. 289–310.

6. For studies of the earth-diver-type myth, see Alan Dundes, "Earth Diver: Creation of the Mythopoeic Male," *American Anthropologist* 64 (1962): 1032 51; and Elli Kaija Kongas, "The Earth diver (Th. A812)," *Ethnohistory* 7 (1960): 151–80.

7. This story is based on the version reported in A. F. C. Wallace, *The Death and Rebirth of the Seneca* (New York: Vantage, 1969), pp. 86–91.

8. For a discussion of the general structure and themes of Navajo mythology, see Sam D. Gill, *Songs of Life: An Introduction to Navajo Religious Culture* (Leiden: E. J. Brill, 1979).

9. Father Berard Haile, *Origin Legend of the Navaho Flintway* (Chicago: University of Chicago Press, 1943).

10. This story is based on the account recorded by Alfred Kroeber, "Cheyenne Tales," *Journal of American Folklore* 13 (1900): 168.

11. This is based on the story in Paul Radin, *The Trickster* (New York: Schocken, 1956), pp. 19–20.

12. See Walter J. Hoffman, *The Menomini Indians*, Bureau of American Ethnology, 14th Annual Report (Washington, D.C., 1896), p. 211.

13. See Morris Opler, *Myths and Legends of the Lipan Apache Indians* (New York: American Folklore Society, 1942), p. 185.

14. For further details, see Frank G. Speck, *A Study of the Delaware Big House Ceremony* (Harrisburg: Pennsylvania Historical Commis-

sion, 1931); Frank G. Speck, *The Celestial Bear Comes Down To Earth* (Reading, Pa.: Reading Public Museum and Art Gallery, 1945); and Mark R. Harrington, "Religion and Ceremonies of the Lenape," *Indian Notes and Monographs* (New York: Museum of the American Indian, Heye Foundation, 1921).

15. For a description of the prayerful act of smoking the pipe, see Joseph Epes Brown, ed., *The Sacred Pipe* (Norman: University of Oklahoma Press, 1953), Chapter 1.

16. Edmund Carpenter, *Eskimo Realities* (New York: Holt, Rinehart & Winston, 1973), p. 59.

17. Bill Holm and Bill Reid, *Indian Art of the Northwest Coast* (Seattle: University of Washington Press, 1975), p. 36.

18. John (Fire) Lame Deer and Richard Erdoes, *Lame Deer: Seeker of Visions.* Copyright © 1972 by John Fire/Lame Deer and Richard Erdoes. Reprinted by permission of Simon & Schuster, a Division of Gulf and Western Corporation.

CHAPTER 2

Nonliteracy and Native American Religions

Among the Omaha, it was a custom at the funeral of a highly respected man or woman for several youths to make two incisions in their upper left arms into which they inserted a willow twig. With blood dripping from their wounds, as an expression of their grief, they danced before the lodge that housed the dead and sang songs with blithe major cadences that suggested birds, sunshine, and lightness. This practice bears the Omaha belief that song is of the spirit and is capable of carrying human thoughts and aspirations to the spiritual world. The songs of the youths cheer the dead as he or she goes from this world into the world beyond life on this earth.[1]

Native Americans commonly view songs, prayers, stories, and other oral events as spiritual forces whose effect and purpose extend far beyond ordinary functions of conveying information or entertaining. Certain words when spoken or sung affect the world, give it shape and meaning. Words can cause pain and suffering as well as create beauty and orderliness.

In several Pueblo stories of creation, the first figure to exist—who, in a sense, has always existed—was Thought-Woman. The world was literally formed as she thought what form it should take. Her partners in creation followed her act of creative thinking by naming those things given form by Thought-Woman. Thus her acts of creation became humanly meaningful through language; names gave distinction and identity to the forms created.[2]

In Central California, thought and speech are personified as the cosmic creators. Many of the creation stories feature a figure who creates the world as he thinks of it or speaks about it. This figure is countered by Coyote, a sort of trickster, whose acts undo or reverse the way the world is created. The story is similar to the Seneca tale of the Twin Brothers discussed in Chapter 1. In this way, the difficult aspects of the human plight, including death, are introduced. In the origin story of the Achomawi, a California tribe, the interrelationship between thought and speech as creators is dramatized thus:

> Apponahah speaks and sings to himself, in his own mind, and thus imagines himself to be the creator of the world. But in the first conversation between Apponahah and Annikadel, who is the personification of speech and was carried as a child in the bosom of Apponahah, Annikadel declares his role in creation by telling Apponahah that thought alone is insufficient as a creator; that thought must be born into the world and that this requires an act of speech. Annikadel proclaims himself as "a man of the air," as "the man who will make all sounds," and thus as the partner of thought in creation. He even declares that he made Apponahah think of all that he had done, thus indicating the dependence even of thought on speech.[3]

For the Achomawi, thought and speech are interdependent creators.

In the Navajo stories of creation, similar roles are played by thought and speech:

> After the people who were to perform the acts of creation emerged from lower worlds onto the mud-covered earth surface, there was a display of the forces that would create life on that surface. It was done by the personification of the objects in the medicine bundle, the womb of life. From the bundle arose a youth and a maiden of incomparable beauty. Their hair was long, and their bodies shone brilliantly. They appeared only this one brief time on earth, but they revealed that they were the means by which all things would be given life; they were to be the very means of life.[4]

The youth and maiden are the personifications of thought and speech, and their names are Long Life and Happiness. Joined together, they are the forces that carry life through time. Even their names are used together by the Navajo as a term that designates the goal of life; all Navajo prayers and songs evoke the names Long Life and Happiness (*sa'áh naghai bik'eh hózhó*), for thought and speech are the forces necessary to create life and maintain the conditions and means by which people live in good health through a long life to attain life's fulfillment by a death in old age.

From these few examples, we can begin to see that acts of thought and speech are of special religious significance to many Native American peoples, although this significance is expressed in a variety of ways. The creative power of the word is reminiscent of the passage in Christian Scripture in the Book of John: "In the beginning was the Word. . . ." Our concern, however, stems from the nature of the communication mode that has underlain the very character of all Native American cultures and religions: unwritten speech images. Until the application of linguists' orthographic (i.e., writing) systems, which permitted the writing of Native American languages, and the invention of the syllabary by the Cherokee man named Sequoya in 1821, Native American languages had never been written. At present, few Native Americans read their own languages, although some tribes like the Navajo have developed a considerable literature published in their own languages. For this reason, we apply the term "nonliterate" to Native American peoples, meaning only that they do not communicate by the use of alphabetic writing. Certainly they communicate in many modes other than the spoken word—as, for example, in symbolic motifs, in art, in ritual acts and gestures, in architectural forms, and so on—but these do not record ordinary human language. It should also be emphasized that the term "nonliterate" does not or should not suggest "illiterate," which designates one who cannot read; or "preliterate," which designates one who has not yet come to the stage of developing writing. Most certainly the term should not be associated with the "unlettered" (i.e., the unintelligent or stupid). Nor should we associate it with romantic notions of a primitive, uncluttered simplicity that we think would exist without writing; the barest acquaintance with Native American speech acts will quickly give the lie to that idea.

We will be concerned in this chapter with how the fact of nonliteracy is significant for understanding various aspects of the religions of Native American peoples. While I do not want to characterize nonliteracy as the single significant distinction between "us" and "them"—a position that would certainly be ridiculous if pressed very far—I nonetheless feel that many intangible aspects of Native American religions can be exemplified and clarified by considering Native American nonliteracy as it relates to, and serves to shape, ideas and forms of expression.

We live in a world in which writing is taken for granted. It is central to our forms of government and economy, our society and material culture (i.e., the things we have), and certainly to our pursuit of knowledge and the ways in which culture is transmitted from generation to generation. No small imagination is required to appreciate and gain a feeling for the character of nonliterate cultures. In order to initiate this act of imagination—as well as to correct certain erroneous associations with the term "nonliteracy" that we might possess—let us look at some examples.

TO BREATHE IS TO MAKE POETRY

In the Amassalik Eskimo language, the word for "to breathe" is the same as the word for "to make poetry," and it stems from the word referring to the soul or stuff of life. The Netsalik group of Eskimo have the same idea, as we see in the famous example of the Eskimo man named Orpingalik. He was a great hunter, archer, kayakman, and shaman. As a shaman, he could engage in the spiritual world with the aid of spirit helpers and guides who had chosen him. He communicated with the spirit world by entering into a state of trance. He called his spirits and spoke with them by singing their spirit songs and by speaking in the special metaphorical language of shamans. His shamanic powers gave him the capability to see game and to hunt successfully, to heal as well as to injure his enemies. He could call the caribou to him through the power of his songs.

> Wild caribou, land louse, long legs,
> With the great ears,
> And the rough hairs on your neck,
> Flee not from me.
> Here I bring skins for soles,
> Here I bring moss for wicks,
> Just come gladly
> Hither to me, hither to me.[5]

Orpingalik's songs and poetry were the base for his success as a hunter and a measure of his stature as a human being. His food as well as his dignity was inseparable from his songs. The Eskimo consider a person's songs as his or her possession, and no one would perform the song or poem of another without permission and compensation for it.

The identity of songs and poems with aspects that are central to life was clearly and self-consciously spoken of by Orpingalik:

> How many songs I have I cannot tell you. I keep no count of such things. There are so many occasions in one's life when a joy or a sorrow is felt in

such a way that the desire comes to sing; and so I only know that I have many songs. All my being is song, and I sing as I draw breath. . . . It is just as necessary for me to sing as it is to breathe.[6]

This identification of song with the very essence of life is also addressed in the sorrowful but poignant statement of a Navajo man who said, "I have always been a poor man. I do not know a single song."[7]

To make song is an act of vitality, of the breath. It is rooted in the heart, the seat of life and center of emotions. It is not only a sign of life, but—as important—an act of life. It is creative in the most primary sense. Orpingalik spoke eloquently of this:

> Songs are thoughts, sung out with the breath when people are moved by great forces and ordinary speech no longer suffices.
>
> Man is moved just like the ice floe sailing here and there out in the current. His thoughts are driven by a flowing force when he feels joy, when he feels fear, when he feels sorrow. Thoughts can wash over him like a flood, making his breath come in gasps and his heart throb. Something, like an abatement in the weather, will keep him thawed up. And then it will happen that we, who always think we are small, will feel still smaller. And we will fear to use words. But it will happen that the words we need will come of themselves. When the words we want to use shoot up of themselves—we get a new song.[8]

There is great depth in Orpingalik's view. It is not the singing of glib songs of joy to celebrate a life of bliss that is never actually realized by human beings. It is an expression of the measure of life with its complexities and overwhelming nature. The mind only grasps life's meaning as it finds a vehicle of expression and manifestation in words, songs, and poetry.

Only these forms can express the incomparable sadness of a mother who loses her son because he has been banished from the community after he killed a hunting companion, as happened in Orpingalik's family. The poem of his wife Uvlunuaq captures her feelings:

> When message came
> Of the killing and the flight,
> Earth became like a mountain with pointed peak,
> And I stood on the awl-like pinnacle
> And faltered,
> And fell![9]

Owners of powerful words are powerful and prestigious in their cultures, but they are also subject to the suspicions of community members when anything goes wrong. Since powerful persons can engage in spiritual affairs with cosmic effect, they are suspect when something goes awry, even when they are the only ones who suffer. The only thing that distinguishes sorcerers and witches from shamanic healers and clairvoyants is the intent or nature of their effects on the world. The powers of one who can bring the dead back to life, heal the ill, or call the animals are dangerously close to those of the witch or sorcerer whose curse or spell can cause illness, deprivation, or even death. The death of another of Orpingalik's sons was judged by the people of his community to have resulted from Orpingalik's attempts to use his powers to kill a rival shaman. They said that the powers of the rival were thus proven the stronger because the efforts of Orpingalik were reflected back upon him, killing his son in an accident.[10]

We may not be much closer to comprehending how the performance of speech acts can create the world or greatly shape it. We may still doubt that speech acts can really do such things. But we should begin to appreciate the strong interconnection among thoughts, words, and life; and we should also begin to appreciate the distinctive character of speech acts. This distinction can be highlighted by contrasting oral and written modes of communication.

Speech is an act that is fragile, impermanent, and intimate. Every speech act is unique, engaging a speaker and a listener in a specific existential situation. All that transpires is the formation of words, symbols of sound, stemming from thoughts. When uttered by the mouth in an act that requires the expiration of breath, these thoughts fill the surrounding space within the power of the sounds. The listeners, including the speaker, receive the sounds through their ears. There remains nothing of the speech act except the impressions it leaves in the memories and effects it renders upon the world. Speech by its nature is very personal. It cannot occur other than from person to person, from speaker to listener. It is an act of the mouth, breath, heart, ear, and mind. A speech event cannot be audited, replayed, or reorganized. There is a limited capacity for recall even in the memory it produces.

Communication in writing is quite different. Writing certainly stems from the mind and often the heart, but it is an act of the hand, usually produced less spontaneously and more slowly and laboriously, since a system of alphabetic symbols and grammatical rules must be engaged to translate the stream of mental symbols into visual images. For this price, however, the written message may be audited, corrected, or erased before it need be submitted to a receiver, a reader. And the reader may reread, reorder, and rephrase it without loss of the original message.

Writing and reading are usually private acts, done by oneself in isolation from others. Reading is physically more directed than is listening. One may much more easily choose to read something than to hear something. Sight is also greatly directed by the viewer, who changes the direction of vision and focuses according to desire. It is said that persons who are blind until adulthood, then given their eyesight by an operation, cannot at first discern one object from another but see only a complex configuration of shapes. This is because they have not yet learned how to look, how to direct the vision toward the desired centers of attention.

Acts of writing are not as fragile as speech acts. Whatever one writes is more or less stable, permanent, and can be read at any time by anyone who knows how to read the language. Negatively, as anyone who has written secret notes in school knows, there is less control on who receives the message. Once it is written, neither the intended receivers nor the context in which the message is intended to be read can always be controlled.

Although these points are rather fundamental, by recalling them we can gain a perspective from which to understand some aspects of Native American religions that are shaped by the situation of non-literacy.

THE COCK AND THE MOUSE

The oral poetry of Native Americans is often described as very stable in its form and composition. Until quite recently, folklorists approached the collection of stories, songs, and prayers in Native American cultures largely with the attitude of checking the occurrence of a certain type of tale or song in an effort to record the lore and oral poetry of a particular culture. Variations of a tale or song were usually not considered as separate incidents; and they were reconciled by putting all of the versions together to form an abstract of what was then considered as the complete story. This tends to give the impression that each Native American people had a fixed tradition of poetry and that actual performance of it was always some corruption or extraction of the full form. Many folklorists have also documented the tremendous stability of various forms of oral poetry over considerable periods of time. Others have shown us that many forms, such as origin stories, songs, and especially prayers, are highly formal, and their exact recitation is rigidly followed. We will deal further with such forms; but first let us look at the potential for immense flexibility, innovation, and creativity in nonliterate modes of communication by means of an incident that occurred during the late 19th century at Zuni.

Frank H. Cushing, an ethnographer, listened to several Zuni men tell folk tales during the summer of 1886. The custom was for everyone to contribute stories in turn. When Cushing's turn came to tell a story, he had to resort to tales that had their roots in Europe. On one occasion, he told them the tale of "the cock and the mouse." A mouse asked a cock to go with him to collect some nuts from a nearby tree. The mouse climbed the tree to gather the nuts, but the cock was unable to fly up to the tree and asked the mouse to throw him a nut. When the mouse did so, the nut hit the cock, breaking open his head. The remainder of the story is a chain of events in which the cock must go to a series of sources in order to cure his head. The total series comes at the end, when the fountain gave the cock some water, which he gave to the forest, which gave him wood, which he gave to the baker, who gave him bread, which he gave to the dog, who gave him two hairs, which he gave to the old woman, who gave him some rags, which the cock needed to cure his head. This tale was then unknown to the Zuni.

Cushing returned to Zuni about a year later. One day in a similar session of telling tales, Cushing heard his own story of a year earlier told by a Zuni. Cushing's recording of the story enables us to examine the remarkable changes it underwent during the period of a single year. While the basic tale remained intact, the story was completely adapted to Zuni culture and bore much of the Zuni world view. The Zuni story was more than fivefold the length of the tale told by Cushing. Apart from a much more complicated relationship developed between the mouse and the cock and the many details added to give the story concrete images associated with Zuni life ways, the conclusion of the story is most significant. When the cock reaches the source of water (in this case a spring), the "Beloved of Waters"—that is, the spirit of water—had a message for the cock:

> Long have men neglected their duties, and the Beloved of the Clouds need payment of due no less than ourselves, the Trees, the Food-maker, the Dog, and the Old Woman. Behold! no plumes [prayer feathers] are set about our border! Now, therefore, pay to them of thy feathers—four floating plumes from under thy wings—and set them close over us, that, seen in our depths from the sky, they will lure the Beloved of the Clouds with their rain-laden breaths. Thus will our streamway be replenished and the Trees watered, and their Winds in the Trees will drop the dead branches wherewith thou mayest make payment and all will be well.
>
> Forthwith the *Takaka* [the cock] plucked four of his best plumes and set them, one on the northern, one on the western, one on the southern, and

one on the eastern border of the Pool. Then the Winds of the Four Quarters began to breathe upon the four plumes, and with those Breaths of the Beloved came Clouds, and from the Clouds fell Rain. . . .[11]

Thus the cock was able to get the bristles from the dog so that grandmother would cure his head. But the Zuni story adds certain explanatory features at the end: The head injury gave origin to the red fleshy cock's comb; the practice by which each party required payment for what it gave coincides with a medicine master requiring payment for his services and medicines, for there is no virtue in medicine of no value; and there are several others.

What this example illustrates is the amazing potential of oral traditions to adapt to the needs and circumstances of the culture. In only one year, the telling and retelling of a new tale was thoroughly adapted to the Zuni world view and made to bear a number of messages regarding proper action, proper conduct, the interrelationship among all living things, the dependence of life on spiritual levels of reality, the dependence of life on proper religious actions, and so on. Folklorists have warned us that it is naive to consider that any folktale has a specific meaning for a culture that tells it. They note that one can find the same basic tale, such as "the cock and the mouse," in cultures as diverse as Zuni and Italy. But while the basic tale remains the same, we cannot help but recognize that it has been greatly adapted to Zuni culture and religion. And doubtless we can learn something about both by considering the tale as it underwent this creative process of oral transmission.

Against the background of this example, we can now look at various factors involved in the transmission of culture among nonliterate peoples. Many material objects are also involved, of course, in the transmission of culture from generation to generation, but speech acts are central. In cultures without written records, the whole history and character of the tradition must be maintained in the memories of its living members. Culture is transmitted in acts of face-to-face communication, a chain of interlocking conversations. Every member of a nonliterate culture must personally and directly experience the tradition because it is largely transmitted in verbal acts. The relationship between symbols and their referents is experienced more directly and concretely. Tradition is more highly socialized because it is communicated only between people in social interaction.

Since the whole of tradition must be held in the memory, cultures commonly adopt various devices to aid the task of remembering. Certain processes are inseparable from the oral transmission of culture.

The forms of speech themselves—stories, songs, and prayers—as well as requirements for the exact recitation of certain speech acts serve to shield the memory from extensive change due to influences of the immediate present. Yet while remembering is essential, forgetting nonetheless has a role: it serves to eliminate anything that becomes irrelevant or meaningless from the tradition. Only what is humanly relevant is retained in the memory; the rest, in time, is forgotten. And since memory is relatively finite, the processes of incorporating present experiences in the tradition must correspond roughly with the elimination of details through forgetting. This dynamic transmission of culture, including the function of remembering and forgetting, can be viewed as a process of digestion. New elements are constantly being added, though these alter the whole character of the culture identity only very slowly in a growth-like process. But as the culture is fed by new experiences, certain aspects of tradition which have become irrelevant may be sloughed off by being forgotten. Their effect, however, is retained in what the culture has come to be.

Story is an ideal form for effecting this process of transmitting culture, as our example has shown. Even the simple tale of the cock and the mouse has, as the Zuni have shown, almost unlimited potential for elaboration and development so that it can support a wide range of symbols as well as provide the underpinning for innumerable aspects of a way of life. It is notable also that the Zuni place the events of the story in primordial time, which is a symbolic way of giving authority to its powers of defining the world. This is also done in the etiological or explanatory elements at the story's end. Statements such as, This is how the cock got its comb, are ways of validating the story. Because it is evident that cocks have combs, it follows that the story is true.

We must now discuss further the notion of meaning. To consider as much as possible of the oral tradition of a people is an essential part of attempting to understand Native American religions, as Chapter 1 attempted to show. But here we run into potential difficulties, for our tendency is to ask questions of meaning. Ordinarily underlying such questions of meaning is the assumption that these oral traditions carry messages and that we need to translate these speech acts into their messages so that we too will know what they mean. After spending much time asking Native American people questions like "What does this story mean?" and feeling by their lack of response that it must have been a stupid question—or having gained answers completely incompatible with the story—I have had to seek ways of understanding how these stories bear meaning and how we can appreciate them. Surely our understanding of Native American religions will be lacking until we resolve this problem, which is also crucial to our understanding of how speech acts can create the world.

Perhaps we can approach an understanding by considering certain olfactory experiences. I cannot smell the odor of juniper smoke without experiencing a series of particular images and feelings related to experiences I had while living among Navajo people. If you were to ask me what the smell of juniper smoke means to me, I would at first be confounded, for such a question seems inappropriate to ask. The smell bears no translatable message, although it has an emotional impact upon me; the experience is meaningful but has no meaning at all in the sense of bearing a message. Listening to music evokes similar sorts of meaning by awakening a certain emotion, often a series of images or memories connected with the music through one's personal and cultural history.

The speech acts in Native American cultures certainly convey information that can be discerned by familiarity with the language and its conventions. But these speech acts have an emotional impact, a significance much more far-reaching. In their performance, they are not simply streams of words whose full significance lies in the information they convey. They are complex symbols, networks of sounds, odors, forms, colors, temperatures, and rhythms. All of these nonverbal features and many more create the patterns through which reality is perceived. They create the moods and goals that give orientation to life. They provide a presence in which actions take on value. Consequently any story, any song, any prayer is a stimulus that frees strings of associated images, emotions, and patterns. To ask what they mean and expect a translatable message is often to ask an inappropriate question. Their significance is inseparable from the whole field of symbols they evoke.

For an example, let us briefly return to the Zuni-revised cock and the mouse story. Upon reading a story like this (note that we don't often *hear* such stories), we are tempted to make the following assessment of the information conveyed. The story tells that people should make offerings of prayer feathers at the cardinal directions around a spring in order to bring rain. Rain, in turn, benefits forests, bakers, dogs, and old women, not to forget chickens. We add that it also answers for the Zuni questions about the origin of cocks' combs. We imply many things by this kind of interpretation, not the least of which is that the Zuni have a burning desire to know the origin of cocks' combs and that they are somehow incapable of scientific investigation to find out, so a fanciful story compensates for their ignorance. This, of course, is a gross misunderstanding of both the story and the whole symbolic process.

Certainly we can correlate the obvious information in the story with cultural practices like making prayer feather offerings; and while this is important to our understanding of the culture, it is not what the story is about and not what is most important to the Zuni. The significance of the story is not even very evident in its words, which are often our only evidence. We must place the story in its context. If we recall that the distinctive aspects of a nonliterate culture are transmitted largely in oral form—that the very view of reality is borne in this way from person to person, from generation to generation—we can begin to understand the creative power of stories and other speech acts. Speech acts are a nearly constant presence in nonliterate cultures from birth to death. They bear the forms, patterns, and shapes—the symbols—that define reality. They literally create the way the world is perceived. A meaningful life is utterly dependent upon them.

PERFORMANCE

So far I have said things about oral traditions in Native American cultures that may appear almost contradictory. I have contended that, from the Native American perspective, certain verbal utterances are creative acts of the highest order. But I have also maintained that the stories do not have their greatest meaning in terms of the abstracted messages they seem to bear. With this tension in mind, let us now turn to the notion of performance, which may help resolve the tension and give us further insight into the nature of the oral aspects of culture that are so important to Native American religious traditions. Let us begin with a Navajo prayer:

> Dark Male Crane,
> I have made a sacrifice to you!
> Coming from the home of dark cloud, from the floor of dark cloud, from the square rooms of dark cloud, along the out-trail controlled by dark cloud, along the trail at the tip of dark cloud, you who travel along with the aid of dark cloud!
> When you have come upon me by means of your feet of dark cloud you have thereby wholly restored my feet! [*Line repeated four times, changing feet to legs, body, mind, and voice.*]
> May the power that enables you to inhale also enable me to inhale, may the power that enables you to exhale also enable me to exhale, may the power that enables you to utter a word also enable me to utter a word, may the power that enables you to speak also enable me to speak!
> May the means that keep your feet in health also keep my feet in health! [*Line repeated four times, changing feet to legs, body, mind, and voice.*]

With its aid you have nicely made me whole again, you have perfectly
    restored me! You have put me back into my former condition!
May you nicely raise me on my feet, do walk me out nicely!
May you cause me to walk about nicely!
May it be pleasant wherever I go!
May it always be pleasant at my front wherever I go!
May it always be pleasant in my rear wherever I go!
Pleasant again it has come to be, pleasant again it has come to be![12]

This "Prayer to the Crane" is repeated addressing several others:
White Female Crane, Blue Male Crane, Sparkling Female Crane,
Wind, Big Fly, Changing Woman, Sun Carrier, Pollen Boy, and
Cornbeetle Girl. Appropriate changes are made for the corresponding
house descriptions and related phenomena. The other prayers in this
ritual process known as Flintway differ only in the names mentioned
and the corresponding phenomena.

We may enjoy the text of this prayer in a number of ways. It is
aesthetically pleasing in its imagery, symmetry, and rhythms. It conveys information understandable to us. The prayer apparently addresses Dark Male Crane in reference to a sacrifice made to it, then
describes the figure coming from its home. It then beseeches Dark Male
Crane to restore the body of the one praying, concluding with a
statement that the restoration has been accomplished and describing
the pleasant experience of being restored. This may seem like a satis-
factory understanding, but we do not realize what we are not seeing
and hearing.

Our knowledge of Native American religions usually comes to us in
the form of written texts, usually in collections of texts or in ethnog-
raphies. First, however, the oral component is completely lost as is the
original language; and second, the text is stripped of the tradition,
separated from its cultural context. In this form it can speak only to our
own sense of meaning and value. We lack the perspective of those who
live it. While an English-speaking Navajo who knows the quoted
prayer might write it down, perhaps to appear just as I have presented
it, this act of writing down a prayer has nothing to do with the
performance of Navajo traditions. Writing prayers is not an act of the
culture. The prayer, when performed as a religious act, is very carefully
placed in a ceremonial context according to an extensive set of rules.
Indeed, it would be difficult to get a Navajo to recite the prayer outside
of a highly specified context. Clearly all cultures distinguish between
talking about certain aspects of the culture's traditions and actually
performing the acts as part of a living religious tradition. Remember
the Navajo man who considered himself poor because he did not have

a single song? We can see that his poverty was not because he wasn't familiar with any songs; but because he had no songs that he could assume the responsibility of performing as religious acts.[13]

It is truly impossible to recreate in writing the experience of a Navajo in the context of the performance of any prayer, for it is an act that engages all of the senses and a lifetime of personal experience in the culture. But even in briefly describing the prayer performance, we can clarify the cultural and religious processes engaged as well as a sense of the experiential dimensions evoked by the performance.

The particular prayer quoted is performed as part of a healing ceremonial known as Flintway, which focuses upon healing accidental injuries—usually internal injuries or those involving a loss of consciousness or vitality. The complex ceremonial may last a number of days and nights and includes many different ritual processes. It occurs in a Navajo hogan that is sanctified by a ritual blessing, which identifies it with the creation hogan built at the emergence place of the Navajo deities upon the earth surface and which replicates the structure of the entire cosmos. The part of the ceremonial in which the prayer is performed involves the ritual bathing of the one who is being treated; the tying of a flint or jewel onto a medicine pouch; and the recitation of the prayer in a litany fashion by the one being treated and the "singer" or official responsible for performance of the entire ceremonial and the knowledge of its ways. Let us look more closely at some of these elements, for they contribute to the significance of the performance.

First, however, it must be noted that this whole ritual process stands against a background of Navajo stories. Flintway originated with the story, which we encountered in Chapter 1, of the healing of the hunter by Gila Monster. This story is known and remembered by the Navajo people; and, in some sense, it is brought before them in the ceremonial performance of Flintway. More generally, however, the ceremonial is performed against a background of the emergence and creation stories. That large context is evoked with the blessing of the ceremonial hogan in the very first ritual act.

In the performance of the ritual bath, songs are sung that refer to Gila Monster and to the powers of his medicine bundle. Songs are sung that identify the bath with the preparation for creation of the world in the beginning. The performance of the ritual bath places the one being treated in the environment of the cosmic forces of creation, purified and sanctified to be the object of these creative forces.

During the prayer, the person being treated ties a flint, a bead, or a jewel onto a medicine pouch as an offering. This is the sacrifice or offering referred to in the prayer. The pouch is identified with the source of the powers that restored the lives of Gila Monster and the hunter in the story. In that story, it was Gila Monster's medicine pouches that performed the restoration. They were described as two human-shaped agates that restored life by stepping over the reassembled body of Gila Monster. When Gila Monster initiated the hunter youth into the knowledge of Flintway, he prepared a representation of his agates for use by Navajos. This was the origin of the Flintway cranebill pouches. The construction of these pouches is significant. They are made by removing the flesh and organs from the bodies of a male and female crane and drying their flesh and organs in the sun. The dried particles from the crane are replaced in the bill in their natural order. Within the skin of the crane that is left attached to the bill are placed large, hollow reeds used as medicine containers. All of the medicines are ritually prepared. One pouch is identified as male, the other female. Only one is used, corresponding to the sex of the person being treated by Flintway.

We may note that the construction of the pouches is a replication of Flintway. The cranes are disassembled and then reassembled in their proper order. They have many other associations with Flintway through the complex preparation of the medicines they contain.

Nor is it without significance that the crane is chosen in association with the central religious object of Flintway. In the songs of Flintway, we find that the crane is of interest to the Navajo in this context because of its migratory habits. It is a bird who always knows where to find the best conditions for life. It is a good parent because it always takes its young to a life-giving place. In another song, we learn that Navajos shout when they see the crane return, for it marks the return of good weather and life-giving conditions to Navajoland. For purposes of Flintway, the crane embodies the power of restoration or return of life.

This outlines only the most dominant features of an exceedingly complex network of associations. But with the understanding that many additional levels exist, we can now turn to the prayer. It is intoned in a litany fashion by the singer and the person being treated; that is, the singer intones a phrase, and the other person repeats it. The sound of Navajo people praying is distinct, in itself evoking many meaningful images to anyone familiar with it, especially to Navajos. The person being treated holds the appropriate cranebill pouch while praying and sits on the floor of the hogan, legs extended, facing east.

Flintway prayers are usually performed in sets; that is, the prayer quoted earlier is intoned a number of times with only minor changes in the wording from one recitation to the next. Each addresses one of two types of figures in the initial line. One type addresses any of a group of deities associated with the waxing and waning of life, seasonal cycles, or diurnal cycles. This group includes such figures as the Thunders, Cranes, and Sun Carrier. Flintway prayers may also address a second type, deities associated with the cause of the injury or illness being treated. If one is injured in a fall, for example, the Earth may be addressed. Other changes in the prayer maintain correspondences with the figures being addressed.

In the first recitation of the prayer, an offering is attached to the pouch at mention of sacrifice in the prayer. The description that follows of the journey of the figure addressed in the prayer refers to the process in the Flintway story when the proper help must be found and brought to the person in need, recalling the efforts of the family of the hunter youth to acquire the help of Gila Monster. At another level, this part of the prayer recalls the life-giving associations with the return of the crane or the thunder. The very journey itself as described is thus a symbol of the return of life.

In the next passage of the prayer, the cure is effected by the identification or close association of the one praying with the one addressed in the prayer. By becoming one with the crane, one obtains the life-giving attributes to which the crane is associated. The identification process is carried out by naming the feet, legs, body, mind, and voice, which are the vital centers of the body in Navajo thought and comprise wholeness as well as holiness.

The conditions of restoration associated with orderliness, wholeness, and mobility are described. The changes in verb tense through the prayer consist of a series that draws attention to the effectiveness of the prayer performance. In this way it is shown that the effects sought by the prayer are accomplished in the very act of performing it.

Let us step back now and consider the power and meaning of the prayer performance; if we can successfully imagine, even in a small way, how the prayer performance engages a Navajo person, we may be able to grasp its creative power. Note that the verbal meaning of the prayer is obvious. For all involved, the prayer bears little news. They know that help is needed and that restoration is desirable. The performance of the prayer, however, is a complex religious act that engages all the senses in response to its smells, sights, acts, sounds, colors, and temperatures. It evokes symbolic images based on personal and cultural history. We can imagine what some of these are in the network of corresponding symbols related to the stories of Flintway and the creation; and to the involvement of certain associations with aspects of the natural world like cranes and thunder.

In performance of the prayer, the set of images and symbols may be carefully channeled to address the very specific needs of the situation motivating the performance. The effect is to identify the specific situation with cosmic processes and primordial events. In Flintway, one not only learns that he or she suffers with a heroic figure but that it is in the nature of life for one to be subject to such sufferings. There are occasions in its very process that life appears to wane. That is the lesson of the crane, of the sun, and of thunder.

The performance is neither simply an instruction nor an imparting of knowledge, although it includes both. More importantly it is the creation of a human experience in which the persons involved may find in the symbolic images insight into the nature of life and character of reality.

CONCLUSION

When Knud Rasmussen was studying the Eskimo in the 1920s, he had an interesting experience. In collecting information on various aspects of Eskimo life among the Iglulik people in the Baffin Bay area, he was quite successful in recording a wide variety of statements about the rules of life, customs, and taboos. But whenever he asked them why they did or did not do these things, he noted that they found this request unreasonable and they could not answer him. Nonetheless Rasmussen continued to ask for justifications. Finally Aua, chief spokesman for the people, took Rasmussen outside where the bitter wind was harshly blowing the snow. He pointed across the frozen landscape and said to Rasmussen:

> In order to hunt well and live happily, man must have calm weather. Why this constant succession of blizzards and all this needless hardship for men seeking food for themselves and those they care for? Why? Why?

Receiving no answer from Rasmussen, he took him to a nearby home. They entered, and Aua pointed out two shivering children huddled beneath skin rugs. Again Aua addressed Rasmussen:

> Why should it be cold and comfortless in here? Kuglo has been out hunting all day, and if he had got a seal, as he deserved, his wife would now be sitting laughing beside her lamp, letting it burn full, without fear of having no blubber left for tomorrow. The place would be warm and bright and cheerful, the children would come out from under their rugs and enjoy life. Why should it not be so? Why?

Again Rasmussen could not answer, and Aua led him to yet another home. This was the home of his sister Natseq, who was very ill. To Rasmussen he said:

> Why must people be ill and suffer pain? We are all afraid of illness. Here is this old sister of mine; as far as anyone can see, she has done no evil. She has lived through a long life and given birth to healthy children, and now she must suffer before her days end. Why? Why?[14]

This event illustrates the fundamental issues raised in this chapter.

Many of the traits that we associate with oral culture, such as its personalization, its immediacy, its concreteness, may also be found in traditions that contain written records and texts. The performance of culture is largely oral whether or not there is writing, and oral characteristics are certainly not absent from written communications. Aua's point was that Eskimos are not peculiar in being unable to discourse on the justification for the nature of existence or certain acts of culture.

This chapter has attempted to show that, while all human beings find it impossible to state the meaning of some aspects of life, these aspects are nonetheless very significant and are felt to be so by peoples of all cultures. What we have learned so far is that literacy has little to do with the ability to express justifications for the nature of existence. Rasmussen was unable to answer Aua's questions about the nature of existence in the Eskimo environment—and doubtless he would have been little more successful at answering such questions in his own Danish environment. But there is another side to this issue. When Rasmussen confronted the details of Eskimo culture, a culture alien to him, he could not resist asking questions like "Why? What does it mean? Why do you do this?" There is considerable evidence that Native Americans and other nonliterate peoples have usually found it unnecessary to ask these kinds of questions.

This suggests that genuine differences exist in processes of thought between Rasmussen and Aua—or, to state it more generally, between nonliterate Native Americans and European-Americans. We must not dismiss this notion too quickly, for it is a key to our understanding of Native American religions.

Differences in modes of thought are relatable to the presence or absence of writing in a culture. While I would firmly hold that all humankind is equal in terms of mental capacity and faculties of reason, I would also hold that writing introduces possibilities for exercising certain modes of thought that are extremely difficult, if not impossible, without it. Writing makes possible a quite different scrutiny of discourse and language events than when writing does not exist. The semipermanency of writing permits and encourages more extensive criticism and analysis. It overcomes the impossibility of juxtaposing language events that occur at widely varying times and places. When writing is present, the capacity of memory and the mental processes of recall and data comparison are not constraints on thought, and the possibilities of certain kinds of intellectual activities are greatly expanded. Certain cultural processes can also occur as a consequence. Based on the analysis and criticism of "texts," one person may write his or her understanding of certain aspects of these documents. These writings, along with the texts on which they are based, can be scrutinized and written about by another person, and so on, thus forming a tradition of criticism and a type of intellection that are virtually impossible without writing. This achievement comes at a price, of course, for writing is often only an abstraction or interpretation of a performed cultural event. Writing may also create a distance between a person and his or her verbal acts.

Returning now to the Eskimo example, we can see that Rasmussen's questions arose out of his own cultural past, the post-Enlightenment tradition of thought characterized in part by the collection, comparison, analysis, and criticism of data from a variety of cultures—an effort that greatly expands the range of human communication and knowledge. But the existence of this kind of enterprise depends upon literacy. Questions of meaning and justification are the stock in trade of this kind of intellectual tradition, for they are necessary for bridging the radical differences in surface appearance.

These differences in mode of thought have nothing to do with mental capacity or with stages in human or mental development. They are strongly related to differences in modes of communication—to the presence or absence of writing.[15]

We must be sensitive to the significance of these differences in modes of thought, for they underlie certain distinctive aspects of Native American religions as well as some of the difficulties we must overcome in order to gain an understanding of these religions. Where European-American thought tends toward analysis and criticism— that is, the breaking down of our subjects of interest so that we may seek principles that hold the pieces together—Native Americans tend toward synthesis and reflection—that is, they attempt to place the object of interest into a broader, often cosmic context—and they note the compatibility that gives expression to the significance of the object. An illness becomes bearable and curable if it is seen as part of the cosmic process. A life is meaningful if its sufferings and joys, defeats and victories, degradations and elevations can be imagined as part of the human story. This process is inseparable from what I have chosen to call religion.

NOTES

1. As reported from the work on the Omaha by Alice Fletcher in *American Indian Prose and Poetry*, ed. Margot Astrov (New York: John Day, 1946), pp. 51–52.
2. Franz Boas, "Keresan Texts," *Publications of the American Ethnological Society* 8 (1928): 221, 224.
3. Account based on C. Hart Merriam, *An-nik-a-del: The History of the Universe* (Boston: Stratford, 1928), pp. 1–6.
4. See Leland C. Wyman, *Blessingway* (Tucson: University of Arizona Press, 1970), pp. 28–30; and Sam D. Gill, *Songs of Life* (Leiden: E. J. Brill, 1979), p. 6.
5. Knud Rasmussen, *The Netsilik Eskimos—Social Life and Spiritual Cultures*, Report of the Fifth Thule Expedition, 1921–1924, vol. 8 (Copenhagen: Gyldendalske Boghandel, 1931), p. 15.
6. Ibid., pp. 16, 321.
7. Willard W. Hill, The Agricultural and Hunting Methods of the Navajo Indians, *Yale University Publications in Anthropology* 18 (1938): 52.
8. Rasmussen, *The Netsilik Eskimos*, p. 321.
9. Dagmar Fruechen, ed., *Peter Freuchen's Book of the Eskimo* (New York: World, 1961), p. 283.
10. Rasmussen, *The Netsilik Eskimos*, pp. 11–12.
11. For a presentation and discussion of this tale, see Alan Dundes, *The Study of Folklore* (Englewood Cliffs, N.J.: Prentice-Hall, 1965), pp. 269–76. The text by Cushing was originally published in *Zuni Folk Tales* (New York: Knopf, 1901), pp. 411–22.
12. Father Barard Haile, *Origin Legend of the Navaho Flintway*, 1943. Reprinted by permission of The University of Chicago Press.
13. For a discussion of performance, see Dell H. Hymes, "Breakthrough into Performance," in *Folklore: Performance and Communication*, ed. Dan Ben-Amos and Kenneth S. Goldstein (The Hague: Mouton, 1975), pp. 11–74.
14. Knud Rasmussen, *The Intellectual Culture of the Caribou Eskimo*, Report of the Fifth Thule Expedition, 1921–1924, vol. 7 (Copenhagen: Gyldendalske Boghandel, 1930), pp. 54–56.
15. See Jack Goody, *The Domestication of the Savage Mind* (Cambridge: Cambridge University Press, 1977), especially pp. 36–44, 150.

CHAPTER 3

Symbols in Action

On a cold, moonless February night, I walked the zigzag road up the mesa to the Hopi village of Shipaulovi. Most of the houses were dark. Light came only from the hatchways atop the several kivas of that tiny village. The yellow lantern light glowing from these partially subterranean ceremonial chambers gave away the places from which the sonorous songs softly permeated the crisp night air. As I arrived at the top of the mesa, a young Hopi man came from a dark house and asked my business. Finding that I had come to see the night dances, he accompanied me to the top of one of the kivas, where we peered through the hatchway to watch the kachinas dancing within. Several other blanket-wrapped young people joined us in the cold.

As the line of awesomely beautiful masked figures sang to the drummed accompaniment, they danced in a stately fashion around the perimeter inside the kiva. Small children, married adults, and elders lined the rectangular kiva on wooden benches. From the middle of the floor beneath the ladder that led into the kiva, a stove spread warmth throughout the chamber.

While we watched the dance, a second group of kachinas approached from below the mesa edge, having finished their dance in a kiva there. Some removed their masks and chatted quietly as they waited for the group of kachinas in the kiva to conclude their performance. One kachina who remained masked would occasionally approach the top of the kiva and call to announce the presence of his group.

After we watched several of these performances, the Hopi youth I had joined suggested that we go to First Mesa some miles to the east, where other night dances were occurring. I agreed, and on this short midnight ride we talked of his family and his future. During our conversation, he turned to the subject of the night dances for a brief explanatory comment, perhaps because I had not asked about them. He said of them only, "What they are doing is mostly a dance for rain." I nodded my head, indicating that I understood what he meant, but I did not.

We arrived at First Mesa, where there was much activity. As the night progressed, more and more teen-agers and young unmarried adults appeared, strolling about the villages. They gathered atop the kivas to watch the dances.

Each kiva in the village is represented by a group of kachinas who rotate from kiva to kiva to sing and dance throughout the night. The view from inside the kiva is remarkably different from that at the hatchway. From within, the night is a continual parade of beautiful, powerful deities who are invited into the microcosmic domain to sing and dance in their sacred way. From the kiva top, the view is rather like that of a play from the backstage wings. One may see the performance taking place, yet from an awkward vantage, and also see the actors preparing their costumes and awaiting their cues to enter the performance stage. But from another perspective, this offstage area is the real world too, and the courting and social activities of the young people who occupy this space are clear evidence of it.

I have thought a lot about the explanation given by that young Hopi man, "They dance for rain," for I have heard it many times from other Hopi and other Native Americans. The statement is simple enough, but it is not so easy to understand. That is partly because dancing is not what we ordinarily consider to be a producer of rain. When we encounter this kind of disparity with our understanding of reality, we usually resort to interpreting it as a symbol. To say that something is symbolic permits us to bracket it, to set aside the questions it immediately raises about the world, so that we can engage it in another way. Commonly we consider symbols to "stand for" something else. They represent something that is not present, but known. We often find in books and on charts a correlation of Native American graphic designs or symbols with what they "stand for." There are symbols for clouds, for lightning, for bears, for beaver, for rain, for mountains, and so on. But even if we were to decode all the symbols of a dancer's costume, for example, what would we have? How would we put them together? What would the costume *mean*? Would we be able to read it like a message? Does this array of symbols of the kachina costume, the songs, the rhythms, the dance, the architecture add up to the message "they dance mostly for rain"? If so, we must surely question the effectiveness of the symbolic language of the ritual performance, for the luxuriance of symbols is far more fascinating than the simple message it would convey.

This leads to the conclusion that while the symbolism of Native American religions is significant, it is not because it bears a message that we can satisfactorily decode and translate. Even if we see that postures, movements, or sounds are imitative of birds or animals, that symbols represent clouds, rain, thunder, or lightning, we cannot find encoded in them a message that seems to justify in any way the elaborate nature of the symbols.

An example will help us come to terms with this problem. Some years ago, a couple of folklorists were interested in the symbolism of the Hopi kachina sash. The sash is a wide, white, woven cotton cloth that is wrapped around the waist of the kachina dancer in such a way that the ends hang down on one side to the length of the dance kilt. On the ends of the sash are colorfully eye-catching embroidered designs. These folklorists pursued their study of the sash symbolism by discussing with a number of Hopi the significance of the embroidered designs. They found general agreement, with some variation correlating with village and mesa. With growing satisfaction that they were coming to understand how the Hopi regard the meaning of the sash, they were surprised when one Hopi told them that they had ignored what was to him the most important part of the sash—the sash itself. He explained that the designs mean little apart from their grounding on the sash; for only when they are on the sash can they be danced.

This suggests to us that the significance of Native American religious symbols is not something we can determine by isolating and decoding particular symbols—that is, by finding out what they stand for—but that they are inseparable from the performance of which they are a part. It also suggests to us that we may not even know where to look for that which is symbolic and significant. What appears to us at first as nothing but the background on which symbols are sewn turns out to be greatly significant from the perspective of the culture to which the symbols speak.

We must come to terms with the way to view and to understand the significance of religious symbols; for otherwise we can scarcely hope to understand much about the aspects of culture that bear evidence of

Native American religions. We will consider some of these aspects in Chapters 4 and 5. Native Americans rarely express their religious beliefs in terms of creeds, religious dogmas, or theologies, but in the highly symbolic forms of dance, ritual movement, and religious objects. These engage the individual at every passage throughout his or her life cycle, and they engage the community in every significant activity that constitutes the community way of life. Native American religions are inseparable from a highly developed symbolism. In this chapter, we will consider several examples of symbols or symbolic processes in order to discuss the nature of Native American religious symbolism. We will find that Native American symbolic processes are inseparable from the symbolic language of place, as discussed in Chapter 1, and from the modes of thought associated with nonliteracy, as discussed in Chapter 2.

RELIGIOUS PAINTINGS

Native American religious artifacts and symbolically painted surfaces and objects are usually considered by outsiders as works of art. They have been extensively collected and displayed in museums and art galleries. Where collection is impossible because of the nature of the artifact, they are reproduced in one manner or another for display. Consequently our principal view of religious symbols that appear in a graphic form has been from an aesthetic perspective, not a religious one. But in viewing from this perspective, we strip the symbols from their grounding in culture; we remove them from the whole milieu of religious beliefs and practices; and consequently we do not even see the background upon which the designs are embroidered. For us they cannot dance.

Sometimes shock or surprise has been expressed with regard to the treatment that Native Americans give to their own creations. Some have wondered why the beautiful, very elaborate murals painted on Pueblo kiva walls were whitewashed and painted over again and again. Some have wondered why sandpainting, the creation of designs in colored sands, is such a temporary art form, for the paintings are destroyed within a short time of their completion. From a perspective in which salability or monetary value is a measure of the aesthetic value, these paintings confound us, for they defy the system by which we would value them. We usually circumvent this transiency on behalf of an artistic perspective by making reproductions that can be permanently displayed and sold. But what of the religious significance of the symbolic acts leading to these creations? Let us consider Navajo sandpainting as an example.

In Navajo culture, sandpainting is a ritual procedure that forms a part of some religious ceremonials performed to cure an ailing person. Constructed on the floor of a ceremonial hogan, sandpaintings depict mythic persons who have a connection with the cause of the illness being treated. These figures must be carefully replicated from the memory of the singer or medicine man; no visual record is kept by the Navajo people, but hundreds of different patterns are known to exist. The finished picture provides a physical form in which the spiritual beings may manifest their presence. When corn pollen is sprinkled on the painting by the singer and the one for whom the ceremonial is being performed, the holy people become present in the sandpainting. In a sandpainting rite, the ailing person walks onto and sits in the *Sacred* middle of the painting, where he or she is identified with each of the *space* holy people present in it. This identification is physically accomplished by a transfer of sands on the medicine-moistened hands of the singer. The sands are taken from the feet, legs, body, and head of each of the sandpainted figures and pressed onto the corresponding body parts of the person sitting on the sandpainting. When this identification is complete, the sandpainting, badly defaced during the rite, is completely destroyed by the singer, who scratches through it with a feather-tipped wand. The mixed sands are then removed and ritually returned to nature.

From the Navajo perspective, each pattern painted in sand is appropriate to only certain of the many Navajo ceremonial ways. Each has its *Symbolic* own story of origin, which in turn is framed by the whole Navajo *action* ideology of creation. No sandpainting can be adequately understood without placing it in these contexts. Also, every ritual performance is uniquely appropriate to the specific cultural circumstances, the felt human needs, that call for it and are often considered in the selection of which sandpaintings will be used. In this way, certain features of a given sandpainting can be emphasized.

The meaning of any specific sandpainting for the Navajo is not discerned by analyzing the distinct symbols within the sandpainting; but rather by how the sandpainting fits into a greater picture that is itself symbolic, created from the experience of hearing the stories, praying the prayers, living the way of life, all of which constitute Navajo tradition. To understand even one sandpainting requires that it be placed within these several levels of its cultural and religious contexts.[1] While that depth of consideration is more ambitious than can be presented here, certain statements can be made about the general religious character of Navajo sandpainting.

During the ceremonials in which sandpainting rites play a major role, the cause of the illness being treated is attributed to impaired relationships with specific life-giving forces in the Navajo cosmos. These life-giving forces are associated with certain holy people whose powers have become directed against the life forces of the ailing person. In the ceremonial cure, rites are enacted to appease the holy people and persuade them to remove their life-threatening influence. But this in itself does not constitute a cure, for the person must be placed again in a state of order modeled upon the creation of the Navajo world. The sandpainting rite is therefore a rite of re-creation, in which the person is remade in a way corresponding to the conditions of his or her ailment. In this rite of re-creation, the sandpainting is the essential vehicle.

From the perspective of the person being re-created, we can see that the person's position—sitting in the center of the sandpainting facing east, toward the opening in the broken circle that surrounds the sandpainting and toward the door of the hogan, facing in the direction of the road of life—is important. This perspective on the painting is unique and cannot be shared by anyone. It is a view of the sandpainting from within it; one is surrounded by it. Only portions of the sandpainting may be seen at any one time, and these only from the center outward. To sit upon the sandpainting and to be identified with the many holy people and cosmic dimensions that are alive in it is to experience the complexity and diversity, the dynamics and the tensions of the cosmos, as represented in the surrounding painting; but also to experience the one point common to all, and therefore to see and feel the unity and wholeness of the universe despite its diversity and tensions.

The illness suffered is an experience of the world at odds with itself, but this experience is cosmicized when the ailing person finds it only incidental to the whole drama of the universe. The illness is overcome when the person realizes that, in some significant places, these tensions and oppositions can be balanced in a unity that signifies good health and order.

We can begin to see, then, that it is not so much the beauty as the use of the paintings—the identification with them—that is central to their religious significance. This helps us understand why the paintings are destroyed after such use. They are not created primarily as objects of

Navajo sandpainting rite

art at all. They are vehicles by which re-creation, health, and beauty in life and the world are achieved. The sufferer finds his or her way to health from within the sandpainting; and in becoming a part of it, it disappears and becomes a part of him or her. The picture disappears in the process of a person coming to know the fullness and unity of the reality it represents. The destruction of the picture corresponds to the dissolution of the tensions and imbalances that gave rise to the suffering.

We often see Navajo sandpaintings reproduced as works of art in books and articles on many subjects; but now, knowing generally how they are viewed by Navajos, we must evaluate the perspective we normally take. We have only representations of sandpaintings drawn or painted on paper or canvas that we enjoy as objects of art. Navajos strictly forbid making representations of sandpaintings, and they are never kept as aesthetic objects. Even the use of sandpainting figures in the sand-glue craft is not approved by most Navajo singers. Sandpaintings must be destroyed by sundown on the day they are made. They are not aesthetic objects; they are instruments of a ritual process aimed at practical concerns. In terms of our visual perspective, we always view sandpaintings from a position that would be directly above them and at such a distance that the whole painting is immediately seen as a whole, with each side equidistant from our eyes. This is completely impossible for Navajos. When a painting six feet or more in diameter or much larger is constructed on the floor of a hogan only fifteen or twenty feet in diameter, the perspective from the periphery is always at an acute angle to the surface. A sandpainting cannot be easily seen as a whole. The most important point of view is that of the person being cured, and this person sees the painting from the inside out because he or she sits in the middle of it. These differences are basic and cannot be dismissed. The Navajo view is inseparable from the significance that sandpainting has for them.

If we can adjust the perspective from which we look at sandpainting to approach nearer to that of the Navajo, we can see that sandpaintings are not the intended products of the creative process by which they are constructed. The product is a healthy human being or the re-creation of a well-ordered world. The sandpainting is but an instrument toward this creative act; and perhaps it is the wisdom of the Navajo to insist that it be destroyed in its use so that the obvious aesthetic value of the instrument does not supplant the human and cosmic concern which it serves.

To recall the hint from the Hopi about the meaning of the symbolism of the kachina sash, we find again that it is not the symbols in isolation, or even the symbols as such, that are significant. It is rather what is done with them; it is the action they perform. The significance of much Native American symbolism is inseparable from the environment in which the symbols gain life and are put into action. Pueblo kiva murals depicted the appropriate background or context in which certain religious performances and actions could take place. They evoked the appropriate moods and atmosphere to frame the important, meaningful aspects of religious activities. As the seasons change, the concerns of religion change, and so must the background.

In a study of the artifacts of Native Americans in the region east of the Rocky Mountains, Dr. Ted Brasser found that the designs on these objects were often self-directed. For example, the designs on the toes of moccasins are oriented to the view of the wearer, not to others looking at the moccasins. He found this self-directed aspect in many objects like birchbark dishes, wooden bowls, drums, woven bags, snowshoes, breechcloths, and pipe bags. He also found that craftsmen confirmed the intentionality of this orientation.[2]

Many museum collections of these objects contain no indication of the proper visual orientation of the objects. This has particular importance for our concern with religious symbolism in the case of effigy pipes. These are pipes with bowls carved in the shape of a figure, a bird, an animal, or a human being. Again, to understand the significance of the pipe from the perspective of the user, we must remove it from the glass museum case and place it back in its religious context. Dr. Brasser found that among the Algonquin peoples, effigy pipes were used as aids in the concentration of thought; that is, they were instruments of meditation. The pipe bowl bore the effigy of the guardian spirit or the familiar spirit of a shaman. It was so placed on the bowl that only when the smoker put the stem in his mouth did he come face-to-face with the representation of the spirit. Hence it was through smoking the pipe, drawing the tobacco smoke through the stem while concentrating on this effigy, that the smoker gained power from his guardian spirit.

Among the Sioux peoples, Brasser found that effigy pipes sometimes took the form of a sitting human male, with the stem representing the penis. Also among the Sioux, he found self-directed effigy pipes of a bear facing the smoker. These were used by shamans whose power to cure and benefit war parties was centered on the spirit of the bear. In their ritual performances, these shamans personified bears, wearing fur costumes and moccasins with bear paws attached.

The point is that the religious meaning of the effigy pipe is inseparable from the act of smoking the pipe, from the relationships of the smoker with the spirit represented on the pipe. It is inseparable from the spiritual transfer that occurred as a result of long hours of concentrated smoking of strong tobacco. The visual perspective was dictated by the use to which the pipe was intended. When not in use, the pipes were not displayed for aesthetic pleasure but carefully wrapped in their pipe bags.

ESOTERIC RELIGIOUS OBJECTS

Tribes over much of North America maintain sacred medicine bundles. These may be associated with a medicine pipe, as among the Northern Plains tribes; the calumet or friendship pipe, as in the Central Plains; or they may be simply a collection of highly sacred objects, as found in many parts of North America. Generally these bundles are not public property, and they are rarely, if ever, publicly displayed. A simple description of the objects in these bundles would scarcely hint that they are held among the most sacred of things. The bundles commonly contain an array of items such as feathers, skins of birds and animals, bones (sometimes, as among the Crow, even a human skull), teeth, herbs and other plants, pebbles, crystal rocks, hair, horse tails, deer tails, pigments, minerals, and many other objects of this kind. The simple, even commonplace appearance of the objects in a medicine bundle belies the importance and sacrality of the bundle.

Bundles of various types have great powers, manifest in many ways for the benefit of the peoples. Bundles may have the power to cure, to be clairvoyant, to call game animals, to assure success in a hunt or war, even to attract a lover. Bundles are commonly considered to be alive and the place of residence of living spirits. They are kept by the most responsible persons and families and cared for constantly. Opening a bundle is ordinarily a complex ritual affair, highly constrained by ritual proscription.

Students of sacred bundles have found that the symbolism of bundle items is often not at all standardized. Bundles used for essentially the same purpose, even within the same tribe, may contain quite different items. Similar items in separate bundles may also be associated with quite different meanings. This variety, not really so confusing, is itself a strong affirmation that these esoteric objects are highly symbolic. It is through the stories of their origin, the histories of their owners and use, the occasions and manner of their use that these objects come to bear significance of a magnitude that infinitely surpasses their commonplace material character. It is in the power they generate, in the significance they evoke, in the awe and respect they command that the symbolic powers of these sacred medicine bundles must be understood and appreciated.[3]

MASKS

A large proportion of Native American formal and public religious acts are masked performances; yet the very words "mask" and "performance" that we use to describe them suggest that these ritual processes are somehow artificial, illusions, enactments of something else being imitated or represented. The word "mask," in almost every sense of its meaning, indicates a covering, disguise, or concealment. "Performance" suggests the presentation of a dramatic work or an entertainment. Yet we are told by native peoples throughout North America that masks are living things, that in masked performances the deities are present. We must take these statements seriously and adjust our perspective to understand these events as creating a reality in themselves rather than being enactments or performances; and that Native American religious symbolism is bound up in this action. Let us examine several examples to help us reshape our point of view.

Seneca False Faces

Very distinctive among Native American masks are the Seneca False Face masks. They are also found among other Iroquois peoples. They are worn by a society of men who perform at the new year's and green corn ceremonies in order to drive out the effects of witches and disease. They bring to presence the forces first shown by one of the twin brothers who created the world. One brother created things to the ease of human life, while his brother kept pace creating nuisances, dangers, and death. The masks make present the power of the nuisance-creating form. They are also used throughout the year for purposes of curing illness.

These distinctive masks are called *gagosa*, which means simply "face," by the Seneca. The "faces" are carefully carved into the trunk of a living basswood tree and removed, if possible, without killing the tree. The masks, which are painted all black or red or both black and red, usually have large eyes made of pieces of metal pierced in the center to form pupils. The mouth and nose are distinctive features, often grotesquely distorted and exaggerated. The mouth often contains huge teeth or a hanging tongue. Each mask is topped with a long hank of hair.

These masks are carved by a member of the Society of Faces and modeled upon a dream revelation. In a man's dream, the appearance of the face of his guardian spirit is revealed, and he carves the mask to make manifest that spirit. The faces when carved are considered to be alive and are treated accordingly by their custodians. When not in use, they are hung facing the wall or are wrapped and carefully placed in a box or drawer. Periodically they are fed by smearing on their lips a thick gruel of parched cornmeal and maple sugar. They are also occasionally wiped with sunflower-seed oil "to keep their skin soft." Old

Masked member of the Society of Faces

masks shine from many applications of oil. Each mask is named and has a personality of its own. They are talked to, sung to, and addressed as "grandfather." The "faces" are considered highly potent, for they manifest the powers of the Bad Twin who, when overcome by the Good Twin at the close of creation, was destined to aid in keeping the health and well-being of human beings.[4]

In this example, we see that the face is not a mask at all, in the sense of being a covering or a disguise. Nor is it false in any sense. The faces are the living manifestation of a type of spiritual being revealed through dreams made manifest in the form of living wooden faces. The wearing of the face is not to cover or disguise the wearer; it is to present and animate the real presence of the spirit.

Looking Through the Mask: The Hopi Case

Among a number of Native American tribes, it is a common practice at rites of initiation into societies that use masks to present initiates with a view they have never had: the view from behind the masks, looking through the eyeholes. Quite often the uninitiated are carefully prevented from knowing about masks. They are never permitted to see masks that are not being worn or performers in costume without their masks. When initiated, they are permitted to look through the eyeholes of the sacred masks. We usually interpret this as a means of educating the initiates to the unreality of the mask; that is, we consider it as showing the uninitiated that, instead of a real being, the masked performer is actually only an impersonation. I think we are wrong in this understanding. Again it is a matter of perspective; the perspective from which one gains the fullest meaning of the mask is not by looking *at* it at all, though this is certainly an essential stage in the process. The full meaning is gained by looking *through* the eyeholes of the mask and seeing the effect it has on the world. That is why it is a privileged view of the initiated. Let us consider two Hopi examples to illustrate this.

Don Talayesva, in his autobiography, told of his participation in the Soyoko ritual, which is aimed at disciplining uninitiated children. In this ritual, monstrous-looking figures come to houses of misbehaving children and demand that the children be given to them as food to eat. This forces the parents to bargain with the kachinas in order to save their children. The children's bad behavior costs the family considerably; and this, along with the fear aroused by the kachinas, serves to encourage proper behavior. Talayesva described a time when he wore the mask of the Giant Kachina and enacted this ritual process. He played his part very well, with great effect on the children. That night Talayesva had a dream, which he described:

> I was tired and restless, and dreamed that I was still a Giant Kachina arguing for the children. I reached out my hand to grab a child and touched him. [Touching a child is strictly warned against for fear of frightening a child to death.] The little one held up his hands to me, crying and begging to be set free. Filled with pity, I urged him to be a good child in order to free himself from the Giant Spirit. I awoke worried, with a lump in

my throat, and bells ringing in my ears. Then I spat four times and decided that if I were ever the Giant again I would have a better-looking mask and speak in a softer voice.[5]

Looking through the mask from inside out, its reality was seen reflected in the faces of the children.

The other example is a comment made by Emory Sekaquaptewa regarding his experience of performing as a Hopi kachina. He says:

> I am certain that the use of the mask in the kachina ceremony has more than just an esthetic purpose. I feel that what happens to a man when he is a performer is that if he understands the essence of the kachina, when he dons the mask he loses his identity and actually becomes what he is representing . . . . The spiritual fulfillment of a man depends on how he is able to project himself into the spiritual world as he performs. He really doesn't perform for the third parties who form the audience. Rather the audience becomes his personal self. He tries to express to himself his own conceptions about the spiritual ideals that he sees in the kachina. He is able to do so behind the mask because he has lost his personal identity.[6]

In this description of the experience, Sekaquaptewa expresses the paradox of how one is at once enacting an impersonation but is also transformed into what he is impersonating. It is described in terms of perspective. One best "sees" the reality that oneself is manifesting by wearing the mask; while looking through its eyeholes, one gains a view from the vantage of the audience and is able to know the reality it presents.

Kwakiutl Masks and the Notion of Place

Much has been written about the importance of the hierarchical social structure of Pacific Northwest Coast tribes and also about the fascinating array of masks used by these tribes. In order to understand the role of the mask, we must understand the Kwakiutl view of reality. It is identified with a grid of relationships defined in primordial times that is eternal. This grid of relationships identifies a fixed number of positions, to each of which belongs a name, referred to as a "seat" or "standing place." Another way of designating the standing places that constitute reality is by crests, which in their highest form are masks. Indeed, the Kwakiutl word *keso* refers to both mask and crest. In Kwakiutl stories, the creation of the family lineages of human beings occurred when the ancestor to the lineage came down to earth, took off his animal mask, and became a human being.

The reality of names, crests, and masks is fixed and eternal, and we may think of it as being animated or given living form by the individual human beings who may temporarily bear the names and wear the masks. From this perspective, only those individuals who obtain a name and the privilege of wearing a mask at ceremonial performances enter into the true reality. Only those individuals have a claim to a truly meaningful role in life. For the Kwakiutl, the mask is what is real, and the wearer of the mask participates in that reality only by virtue of the privilege of wearing the mask.

Once again we see that the mask is not a covering or a disguise at all, but an appearance of that which is at the deepest level of reality.[7]

Conclusion

From these examples, we must adjust our thinking about Native American mask symbolism. Masks are symbolic not because they cover up or disguise; they are symbolic because of what they make present: the spiritual reality. Masks cannot be translated or decoded because their meaning is inseparable from what they make present— which, apart from the masks, could not be observed or expressed. We must see that it is the inexplicability of the human capacity even to grasp the reality of the sacred, much less to serve as its agent of manifestation, to which the symbolism of masks gives full expression.

CLOWNS: MASTERS OF SYMBOLISM

A masked appearance is noteworthy to the observers because it contrasts with ordinary appearances. Just this extraordinary aspect of the experience signals that it is symbolic; that is, that it speaks in ways other than the ordinary. It is in their genius for portraying the most extraordinary that clowns find their role, and therefore we can see them as masters of religious symbolism. Unfortunately we have not been quick to recognize the important religious role of Native American clowns, despite repeated testimony by Native Americans to their sacredness. Perhaps this was because early observers were so threatened and shocked by clown behavior, commonly seen amidst the most sacred festivals and places, that they were incapable of seeing or believing what they were told.

Throughout much of the 19th and early 20th centuries, Native American clowning was reported by outsiders in descriptions that scarcely hid the observers' disapproval of the actions they witnessed. Their use of Latin or English euphemisms to describe the explicit sexual and physical antics of the clowns doubtless reveals as much about their own religious and cultural values as about the Native Americans they

Pueblo striped clown

were observing. But clowning is an activity deeply embedded in Native American religions; and since our difficulty in seeing clowns as religious is linked with the very character of one aspect of Native American religious symbolism, we must consider this fascinating subject.

Native American clowns are many and varied. One possible way to discuss clowning is to consider several of the modes or types of symbolism they may utilize in their performances. Certainly no clown performance is restricted to any single type of symbolism; but clown performances will often tend to one or another type.

Being Contrary

One symbolic mode commonly taken by Native American clowns is
that of being contrary; that is, doing everything just the opposite of the
way it is ordinarily done. Perhaps the best known of the clowns who
are masters of this symbolism is the Sioux *heyoka* who rides backwards
on his horse, puts his boots on the wrong feet, walks backward, wears
heavy clothing in the summer and goes naked in the winter, says "yes"
when he means "no," and so on. The *heyoka* is not a deviant to be
scoffed at and removed from society; he is the receiver of a vision of the
Thunder Being, the personification of the cosmic principle that gives
meaning and definition by countering the principle of normalcy. The
heyoka is like the mask that makes the Thunder Being visible on earth.
There is plenty that is humorous about the *heyoka* within his own
society; but inseparable from the contrary behavior is the threat of
disorder it poses, a threat like the destruction of the Thunder Being
who brings storms and lightning. Yet the Sioux, when commenting
about this aspect of *heyoka*, point to the creative results gained even
from such threatening experiences. Thunder and lightning threaten
destruction, but they accompany the refreshing rains of the storm.
Likewise while the contrary behavior of the clown threatens disorder,
the values of normalcy are defined by contrast with the absurdity of the
clown behavior.

The Forbidden

A major symbolic role of Native American clowns is the portrayal of
all things that are forbidden, unnatural, or considered to be inhuman.
Nineteenth-century observers were horrified by some of the actions of
Pueblo clowns. They sometimes eat and drink dirt, excrement, urine,
live mice, sticks, stones, and whatever is considered defiling. They
appear nude and engage in the most explicit sexual activities, even in
the most sacred places during public performances. Just before 1900,
for example, Alexander Stephen, who was living among the Hopi,
reported that a male clown dressed as a woman came into the plaza
with a wash basin and began to wash her legs, spreading them to
reveal beneath the skirt a huge false vulva, a sight that brought much
laughter from the spectators. Another clown then appeared wearing a
large false penis made from the neck of a big gourd. He approached the
"female" clown and, taken with her sexual features, engaged her in
vigorous simulated copulation. All of this occurred on a sacred shrine.

Examples of clowns engaging in ordinarily forbidden activities could
be multiplied almost endlessly. There is more than the symbolism of
opposites manifested here; and there is more than the symbolization of
the interdependence of destruction and creation. This action gains its

power from the symbolism of pollution and dirt. Mary Douglas's study of this kind of symbolism in her book *Purity and Danger* is enlightening. Although she does not discuss Native Americans or clowns, she helps us understand how Native Americans can describe these clown activities as very sacred and as having such great powers that they may cure people and help the community in pursuit of its way of life.

Dr. Douglas asks the question that has surely crossed the minds of many observers of these defiling clowns: "Can there be any people who confound sacredness with uncleanness?" She concludes that such a confusion is utterly senseless and therefore that we must come to understand the symbolism of dirt and pollution, the symbolism engaged when the clowns perform these almost unspeakable acts. She reminds us that dirt (and subsequently forbidden actions) is created as a by-product of the creation of order. There is an initial state of nondifferentiation; that is, when nothing was distinguishable from anything else. The process of creation, which requires differentiation, results in meaningful order, but dirt as a product of the same creative process constantly threatens the distinctions being made. Dirt is like the category "weed"; it is a thing out of place, a "petunia in an onion patch." For a thing to be recognized as dirt, one must have a very clear notion of the character of order, the requirements of proper place, and the compelling significance of that created order. Even beyond that, dirt or pollution has the ability to evoke, albeit often by revulsion, an experience of the powers that bring order into the world. The highly evocative powers of a polluting act bring one symbolically into touch with that which is fundamental to creation, that which gives compelling significance to a created order. Dirt, like formlessness, is symbolic of the beginning stages of creation and growth as much as of decay. And that is its significance.

To engage in the defiling acts of this type of clowning is not simply to manifest the counterforces that, when balanced, make the universe cohere, as do the contrary clowns; it is to present the experience of chaos, of no order at all, of nondifferentiation. The great danger risked in these activities is accompanied by the acquisition of power—for in transgressing such ominous boundaries, the clowns engender the very forces of differentiation that distinguish order from chaos and thereby create a meaningful world. There is a deep paradox here, and its inexplicability is precisely the symbolism that these clown masters create—not only to give it expression, but to engender the creative forces with which they dare to deal. Defiling clowns are often considered even more powerful than the shamans.[8] Importantly these defiling acts of sacred clowns could never be done apart from the appropriate ritual framework. Only in this framework can the engendered powers be controlled and turned ultimately to a creative purpose. Such acts performed out of the bounds of religious structures would be destructive and completely untolerated.

The Portrayal of Human Folly

Native Americans reflect upon the character of human beings through clowning, thereby gaining important insight, as well as a certain amount of chastisement and instruction, from enjoyably observing the clowns' portrayals of human folly. This kind of symbolism involves the expression through exaggeration of the needs and drives distinctive of human beings. These acts are not contrary to the ordinary, nor are they a defilement or pollution. They are simply an exaggeration, like a cartoon. Clowns are well known for being gluttonous, willing to do anything for something to eat. Clowns also portray failure to see the obvious and play the fool as a result. They learn only by making the same mistakes over and over again. They are greedy to the point of destroying what they desire in an unwillingness to share. Their sexual needs are great and not at all disguised. Clowns often approach people in the audience with sexual gestures and engage in all sorts of sexual innuendos. They enact skits portraying aspects of human sexuality. Such clowns often strike a marked contrast to the concurrent appearances of the masked deities. Many examples could be given in which the clown performances present an image of the difficulties that human beings encounter, as a result of their nature, in their attempts to attain human fulfillment.

When Humor Turns to Fear

In all clown performances, the distance between the clowns and the audience is a key to the effect they achieve. Even for outsiders, clown antics are outrageously funny so long as they can be observed at a comfortable distance. To see clowns engage in sexual activities with one another or approach an observer in a mocking or threatening manner is very funny. I once saw a group of Hopi clowns approach an Anglo observer sitting on a chair in the dance plaza. These seats are unspokenly reserved for the older women. Four clowns grabbed him, one each on his arms and legs. They lifted him high in the air again and again, finally leaving him lying on his back on the ground with his arms and legs flapping like an overturned turtle. But such a funny sight as this turns to fear if one happens to be the object of such activity or is drawn by the clowns into unwilling participation.

In the matter of this delicate dividing line between humor and fear, clowns are also masters. To be only threatening would greatly limit the impact of clowning, eliminating all the subtleties of their humor. Yet to eliminate the element of fear altogether would be to truncate the symbolic significance of clowning; it would then be mere acting. When that line from humor to threat is crossed, it serves as a reminder that the actions are not symbolic in the simple sense of encoding messages. They are symbolic in the much deeper sense of evoking emotions, of fostering the powers that shape and could also destroy the world.

SYMBOLIC MATERIALS IN ACTION

As with the clowns, much attention has been given to Native American sacrificial rites like the widespread sun dance, in which many individuals shed blood as part of the ceremony; and the Skidi Pawnee sacrifice to Morning Star, in which a captive girl was periodically killed.

The Skidi Pawnee sacrifice apparently occurred only when Mars was a morning star. It originated in a dream, in which Morning Star appeared to a Skidi man and directed him to capture a sacrificial victim. This man would capture a girl from an enemy village and return her to the chief of the Morning Star village, where she was treated kindly until her sacrifice. When the time came for the sacrifice, ceremonies that lasted for four days were performed. They concluded on the fifth morning with the bloody sacrifice of the girl.

Morning Star was commemorated with a sacred bundle that held many ceremonial objects used on this occasion. During the first three days, songs were sung describing the exploits of Morning Star. Tobacco smoke and dried meat were offered to the Morning Star bundle. The girl was purified with smoke, painted red, and dressed in a black costume that had been kept in the bundle. Her captor was also dressed in a costume, which came from the bundle, by means of which he personified Morning Star. Cosmic symbolism appears throughout the ceremonies. On the last evening, the priests sang a song describing the journey of the Morning Star in search of the Evening Star, while one of the priests danced with his war club about the lodge, obliterating the four circles inscribed on the floor to represent the four world quarters. A series of songs of Evening Star were then sung, during which counting or tally sticks from the bundle were laid down marking the progression of the victim from the human world to the divine world of celestial beings.

Then a priest painted the girl's body black on one half and red on the other, and they set out for the place of the sacrifice. In that place a scaffold consisting of two uprights and five crosspieces had been erected. Each part had cosmic symbolism. The girl was lifted onto the scaffold and tied into position so that as the morning star arose, her captor (personifying Morning Star) approached her. With a sacred bow and arrow, he shot her through the heart while another man struck her on the head with a sacred war club. The officiating priest immediately opened her breast with a flint knife and smeared his face with her blood, while her captor caught the falling blood on dried buffalo meat and corn seeds. Then all male members of the tribe approached her and shot arrows into her body.

One priest remained after the others had dispersed to take down the body and lay it on the ground, head to the east. The blood-soaked buffalo meat was burned under the scaffold as an offering. Finally the priest sang songs describing how the body would be eaten by various animals and consequently be returned to the earth.[9]

In this sacrificial rite, reminiscent of the bloody sacrifices of the Aztec in Mexico, a large group of symbols was engaged to reenact the history of the people who find their identity and source of life identified with the Morning Star bundle. But no symbol here is so potent as that of blood. Blood is not a substance that can be kept in a bundle or used passively; blood is an active symbol and can be nothing else. To shed blood in sacrifice is a symbolic act but not a passive or simply representative one. The bloody sacrificial rites once performed by the Skidi Pawnee must be understood as engendering powerful symbols that express the inexplicable interdependence of life and death: a relationship symbolized by the rising and setting of the red planet Mars; the chase of the Morning Star by the Evening Star where the death of one signals the life of the other; the life and death of the sacrificial victim; the living of humans by the dying of animals; the consumption of the victim's body by animals; and the blood, which signifies the substance of vitality as well as death. Blood as a substance means little until it is brought into action and transformed into a powerful symbol in this rite of sacrifice. Then it becomes so potent as to be central to the commemoration of the sacred history of a people and to give expression to the most profound and inexplicable of cosmic principles.

But we must see that blood's symbolic significance can be understood only when it becomes an active symbol in a symbolic field of experience. For example, we can appreciate the fact that the blood of menstruation outside a cultural context is symbolically ambiguous. In some cultural contexts, it is the most polluting and threatening of substances; the menstruant is isolated from others, especially potent men, a practice common among Algonquin tribes. But the blood of menstruation can just as well symbolize the powers of fecundity. In this case, the menstruant is in possession of powerful medicine and contact with her is sought by the ailing that they might be cured, by children that they might grow and learn, and by the aged that they might continue to live. This attitude is common in the Southwest.

Many substances and materials have widespread use as religious symbols in native North America. Like blood, they are often associated with life and capable of mediation between categories that are clearly distinct but mutually interdependent. Perhaps no substance, for example, is so widely used for its religious significance as tobacco. It is associated with food, with the breath, with the lungs and heart. In the act of smoking, the tobacco enters into the vital processes of human beings by being taken into the lungs and is then exhaled to rise to the sky and dissipate. It is often associated with acts of prayer and mediation between the human and other-than-human world.

Pollens of corn and other plants are widely used as religious symbols, especially among agricultural peoples. Pollen is the substance that moves between male and female plants to produce fertilization. As such, it is inseparable from life and fertility. Its capacity and function as a mediator constantly associates it, like tobacco, with prayer and communion. Pollen is strewn or eaten in gestures of blessing.

The costumes and rituals of Native Americans often involve the extensive use of feathers. Among many tribes, nothing is more sacred than feathers. Feathers can scarcely be symbolic apart from images of motion, flight, air, and the sky. The types of birds from which feathers can be collected and the habits and character of those birds provide an endless potential for religious symbols.

CONCLUSION

Let us end this chapter by recalling the statement I was told by a Hopi in explanation of the Hopi dances: "They dance mostly for rain." We must now recognize that this statement is almost as highly symbolic as the dances themselves. I do not believe that this statement was an attempt to dismiss the complexity of the lavish religious symbolism by relegating it to some mundane concern such as rain. The significance of the statement and the ritual dances to which it referred cannot be

Symbols represent that which can't be explained: the process of the world, the elicitors, the movement of power

expressed in terms of a message. Their significance must be seen in terms of the highly symbolic religious processes that they engaged. The dances are deeply rooted in the traditions of the people, their history, their stories and poetry, their whole way of life. This is also true for a wide range of Native American religious symbols, as we have shown in the examples throughout this chapter. Religious symbols do not simply comment on life or commemorate things past or entertain—yet they do all of these to some extent. They set off a process by which life and a way of life for a specific people gains its significance. While one cannot decode the message of religious symbols, they serve to make life itself significant, and they do so by their ability to grasp, to express, and to engender the transcendent, as well as the paradoxical and inexplicable. If one could completely and efficiently explain what a symbol communicates, the symbol would be unnecessary; but precisely because that cannot be done, the symbol is significant and creates significance. Thus the symbolic process does not simply encode messages. It evokes the fundamental structures and patterns from the tradition and thereby establishes a meaningful form in which the future may unfold.

We can finally see that, in terms of the Hopi perspective, dancing is the symbolic process through which the structures and patterns of Hopi culture are defined and expressed. Through the symbolic movement of dance, culture and its underlying religious principles are effected and brought into being. This is nothing short of giving life, an act so appropriately symbolized in the desert regions of northeastern Arizona by the essential rain.

For only the Hopi can the dance create the Hopi reality and way of life. Hence we can never know, in the same way a Hopi knows, the significance made possible by these dances. But we can appreciate and understand that the dances create life, and we can even glimpse something of the significance that the Hopi symbols evoke when they are danced.

NOTES

1. I have in this way discussed the Whirling Logs sandpainting; see Sam D. Gill, "Whirling Logs and Coloured Sands," in *Native Religious Traditions*, ed. Earle H. Waugh and K. Dad Prithipaul (Waterloo, Ontario: Wilfrid Laurier University Press, 1979), pp. 151–63.

2. See Ted J. Brasser, *"Bo'jou, Neejee!" Profiles of Canadian Indian Art* (Ottawa: National Museum of Man, 1976).

3. For sources on sacred bundles, see Åke Hultkrantz, *Prairie and Plains Indians* (Leiden: E. J. Brill, 1973), pp. 21–25; George Dorsey, *Traditions of the Skidi Pawnee* (New York: Houghton Mifflin, 1904), pp. 1–14, 55–57; and Clark Wissler, *Ceremonial Bundles of the Blackfoot Indians*, Anthropological Papers, vol. 7, part 2 (New York: American Museum of Natural History, 1912).

4. Anthony F. C. Wallace, *The Death and Rebirth of the Seneca* (New York: Vintage, 1969), pp. 79–93.

5. Don Talayesva, *Sun Chief: The Autobiography of a Hopi Indian* (New Haven: Yale University Press, 1942), p. 184.

6. Emory Sekaquaptewa, "Hopi Indian Ceremonies," in *Seeing With A Native Eye*, ed. Walter H. Capps (New York: Harper & Row, 1976), p. 39.

7. See Irving Goldman, *The Mouth of Heaven: An Introduction to Kwakiutl Religious Thought* (New York: John Wiley, 1975), pp. 62–63, 228.

8. For a discussion of pollution and taboo, see Mary Douglas, *Purity and Danger: An Analysis of Concepts of Pollution and Taboo* (Baltimore: Penguin, 1966), especially pp. 188–210.

9. See G. A. Dorsey, "The Skidi Rite of Human Sacrifice," *Proceedings of the International Congress of Americanists* 15 (1907): 65–70; and Ralph Linton, "The Origin of the Skidi Pawnee Sacrifice to the Morning Star," *American Anthropologist* 28 (1926): 457–66.

CHAPTER 4

Roads of Life

For most Native Americans, life unfolds in the midst of a landscape endowed with the symbolic significance that provides orientation and direction. The mountains, the cardinal directions, the celestial bodies, and many other natural features commonly reflect complex religious symbolism. The cycle of human life, the journey from birth to death, is brought into line with cosmology by being depicted as a process of movement within the landscape. Life is a road one travels, and the proper course for that road is often defined through cosmic symbolism.

The road of life is often described as an orientation. The Hopi, for example, consider the life orientation as from west to east. This is the direction in which the rain clouds, which are identified with kachinas and dead ancestors, move to bring the life-giving rain. This is the direction in which the Hopi ancestors traveled when they migrated to their present homelands from the place of their primordial emergence onto the earth surface. It is the direction one faces to greet the sun when it arises from its night home. The Hopi believe that an unwell person must reorient his or her mind to an easterly direction; the ill are accused of thinking in a westerly orientation.

The road of life is graphically depicted as a labyrinth by the Pima and Papago of the southern Arizona deserts. This symbolic design is often woven as a pattern in baskets. It consists of a circle, in the center of which a small circle represents the earth. Beginning a short distance from the earth in the center, four lines radiate in each direction, but they encircle the center in a fashion that concludes with the ends of these lines enclosed within the pattern formed by other lines. The result is a single path labyrinth (see illustration). The directional lines are associated with the four winds, messengers of the culture hero and creator deity *I'i'toi,* who is represented in humanlike form at the entrance to the maze. The labyrinth depicting the road of life thus portrays the difficulties of life, its conflicts, and its confusions, but it goes beyond this. The symbol of the labyrinth shows that life is directed toward the center and that one who follows the path under the direction of *I'i'toi* will find the goal in the center despite the unavoidable complexities and sorrows in life.

Peyote religion, the religious practices organized under the name Native American Church, has become a widespread pan-Indian religion.[1] The rituals of Native American Church meetings depict the road of life according to the peyote way as a line drawn on a crescent-shaped altar. At the center of the road, in the middle of the altar, is placed a large, perfect peyote cactus button, which represents Chief Peyote, the principal spirit or deity engaged in the peyote religion. Further discussion of peyote religion will follow in Chapter 6.

For the Oglala Sioux, the road of life is distinguished not only by its directional orientation, which is from north to south, but also by a red color designation. North is the direction associated with purity and south with the source of life. Thus an orientation along this axis is the proper orientation for life. The red road is in opposition to the east-west orientation, which is described by the Sioux as the blue or black road. The follower of this path is thought to be distracted, ruled by his senses, and selfish.

We may recall from examples already given that the Delaware-Lenape depict the road of life in their Big House ceremonies and the Navajo in their common symbolic pattern of the broken circle.

Quite often we are reminded that Native Americans do not isolate a category of culture or human activity that they specifically call "religion." Few words exist in Native American languages that translate very closely to the word "religion." We have learned that religion permeates all aspects and domains of Native American life and culture. Still, this does not necessarily make Native American cultures unique among religious cultures in human history. Further, we must certainly not dismiss the many formal religious occasions that are invariably distinguished in the languages of Native Americans. There is a series of life crisis passages, such as the process of birth and puberty, which are celebrated and enacted through formal ritual activities. These occasions are distinct moments in the culture. Together they often com-

Pima/Papago labyrinth

prise much of what we can most clearly identify with our category religion. These formal religious activities are often complex and serve a variety of functions. Through them, the individual gains knowledge of tradition, access to the privileges of performing certain vital roles in culture, and access to the powers upon which successful progress toward life goals can be made.

In this chapter, as we focus upon the religious life of the individual person in Native American cultures, we will commonly find that life is lived as a journey along a road well charted and carefully directed by the religious tradition. Many elements in Native American religious traditions are engaged at each moment in the process of life from conception to death. We may think of this as a nurturing ambience as well as a narrow and precarious path. Further, while this ambience guides and directs the actions of each person, making his or her life meaningful from the smallest to the grandest terms, it also provides the person with access to processes of individuation; that is, to the way in which an individual is a creative, distinct human being within a community joined together by a common religious tradition.

Even a modest summary of any of these religious events is impossible here, for the variety of data in North America is immense. Consequently we will look at some select examples in this chapter to illustrate the many ways in which a religious tradition may inform and activate the religious life of persons within the culture. Our examples, which should not be considered representative, will be generally ordered to correspond with significant points or activities in the process of the life of an individual person. This approach should serve as an introduction to the various kinds of elements that may be present in any Native American religion, as well as suggest how these elements function religiously and culturally.

BEGINNING THE JOURNEY

Human Origins

In the era of creation before human beings peopled the land of the Navajo, Changing Woman became the personification of the source and powers of life. The world was cleared of monsters through her benevolent and thoughtful acts and made ready for the origin of the Navajo people. When all was ready, Changing Woman took residence in a home especially prepared for her. It is located in the ocean beyond the western edge of the land. Her house has four rooms, each of which corresponds to a domain and season of the world. It is the nature of Changing Woman, as her name suggests, to change from youth to adolescence to adulthood and then to old age in a never-ending cycle. As she changes through the four stages of life, she takes residence in the room of her house that corresponds to her respective life stage. In her home, Changing Woman lives in correspondence with the earthly life cycles of the people to whom she gave origin.

In the creation era when the world had been put in place, Changing Woman began to think about what should be done. She thought of the creation of human beings. She went to the first of the four rooms of her house and there rubbed off the outer layer of skin from her chest. She mixed this with pollen and formed it into a ball, which she placed in a basket on the side corresponding with the room she occupied. Then she proceeded through the other rooms, rubbing balls of skin from her back, her right arm, and her left arm. She then covered the basket and stepped across it four times, whereupon from the basket arose four men and four women, the progenitors of the first four Navajo clans. She dressed the men in fabrics and the women in jewels. Then, to distinguish them as human, she gave them speech and instructed them to tell stories to each other. She continued to instruct them in all the ways of human beings. She told them of the holy people and how they might be contacted. She told them of the appropriate duties and activities for men and for women. She told them of the special concerns to which each of the clans should direct their attention. She instructed them about their houses, their fields, their animals, and their water. At dawn the next day, she sent them on their way to the land she had prepared for them. For the Navajo, the road of human life is thus coincident with the way of the entire world.

It is not unique to the Navajo that human life should have its model established in the era of cosmic creation; nor that human life corresponds with cosmic processes. As we have already seen in many ways, Native American religious traditions inform human beings of the meaning of the world in terms of symbolic correspondences between the ordinary and the cosmic. The division of sexes, the organization of clans, the entire social structure, and the life process of individuals are not isolated from cosmic processes; indeed, they are one and the same.

The origin of human beings is not always a part of the stories of the origin of the world—but where it is included, we often learn much about the concept and way of life and the notions of destiny held by the people of that tradition. Many Native American hunting peoples, for example, trace the origin of human beings to a descent from animals or from the progeny of an animal-human marriage. More common among cultivating peoples are stories that do not recount the creation of human beings but are concerned with how they came to the present world. Here we may recall our discussion of the Zuni example in Chapter 1. For a people to have their way of life established by deities or creators in the primal era, the meaningfulness of life and the promise for its fulfillment are assured. Such an origin also establishes life as a religious activity, for it is in accordance with the creators and with the cosmic processes that they originated and may continue to direct.

Conception and Birth

The sexual act of procreation and the period of pregnancy is not a time usually celebrated by ceremonials of any extent; but it is often seen as a period of intense regulation of the activities of the mother, in particular, but sometimes also of the father and other relatives. Food, social relationships, work, even events that the mother and father witness are often considered to have an effect on the health and destiny of the new life. It is common for people who suffer illness or strife, even when well into adulthood, to attribute it to incidents that occurred while they were carried in their mother's womb. In light of this attribution, it is notable that many Native American autobiographies begin with an account of the prenatal period and birth events. In his autobiography *Sun Chief*, Don Talayesva, a Hopi, described the incident in which he was conceived as twins—but because the Hopi do not receive twin birth as a happy event, his mother underwent a rite in which the twins were joined together; in his words, they were "twisted into one."[2]

Ceremonies and prayers are in some cultures given for the expectant mother as her time of delivery approaches to assure her and her child good health.

Birth is an event carefully regulated by tradition, but rarely is it an event for public ceremony. That is more likely to occur on the occasion when the infant and its mother are presented to the community and to the deities. This may occur after a period of confinement. Special prayers, such as the following one from Zuni, may be said to bless the newborn. On the eighth day of the infant's life, its head is washed by its father's female relatives and corn meal is placed in its hands. Then, at the moment of sunrise, it is taken out of doors and faced to the east. As the following prayer is spoken by the paternal grandmother, corn meal is sprinkled toward the rising sun:

> Now this is the day.
> Our child,
> Into the daylight
> You will go out standing.
> Preparing for your day,
> We have passed our days.
> When all your days were at an end,
> When eight days were past,
> Our sun father
> Went in to sit down at his sacred place.
> And our night fathers

Having come out standing to their sacred place,
Passing a blessed night
We came to day
Now this day
Our fathers,
Dawn priests,
Have come out standing to their sacred place.
Our sun father
Having come out standing to his sacred place,
Our child,
It is your day.
This day,
The flesh of the white corn,
Prayer meal,
To our sun father
This prayer meal we offer.
May your road be fulfilled
Reaching to the road of your sun father,
When your road is fulfilled
In your thoughts (may we live)
May we be the ones whom your thoughts will embrace,
For this, on this day
To our sun father.
We offer prayer meal.
To this end
May you help us all to finish our roads.[3]

Other moments early in the life of an infant, such as the loss of the umbilical cord, the first laugh, and the occasion of naming are also commonly given special acknowledgment in North America in the form of ceremony and feast.

Naming

Native American views of names and the process of naming are expressed by N. Scott Momaday, who quoted his grandfather as believing that "a man's life proceeds from his name, in the way that a river proceeds from its source."[4] With identity tied so closely to name, the selection and bestowing of names are often matters of ceremony and complex customs. Among many cultures, a child's name is chosen to identify him or her with an admired elder or ancestor; or may serve even to reincarnate an ancestor. The name is sometimes identified with the soul and hence with the very force of life. Names are also identified with stations of reality, as in the Kwakiutl culture previously described. The Eskimo reveal a similar view, identifying a name with the reality to which it is attached in a practice that accompanies the birth. As the mother is about to deliver, an elderly woman is called in to pronounce as many eligible names as she can recall. The child comes forth from its mother when it hears its name being called.

Many Native American cultures do not consider an unnamed child to be fully alive—or, put differently, to be fully human. If a child dies before it is named where this belief prevails, funeral rites may either be greatly abbreviated or not done at all. It is believed that the life force will soon reenter the mother's womb to be born again.

As will become increasingly evident in our discussion of the moments in Native Americans' journeys through life, the life road is not simply a series of distinct steps, each leading to the next. The life road is rather a way; and as one proceeds along the road, he or she accumulates the knowledge of—and thus gains identification with— this way of living. For example, the act of naming has major significance because it is much more than a once-used custom by which a person gains a label. In many Native American cultures, naming is a practice engaged at many points throughout life. One may receive names as awards for acquiring prestige. A name may be given a young man after returning from his first successful hunt or war party or after completing initiation into a particular society or order. The Choctaw referred to all boys, until they earned a name, by a name that would translate literally as "Choctaw without a name."

Nicknames are often used to identify distinctive personal features or characteristics, but they may also be used to ridicule or criticize the actions of any person. Pronouns are commonly very complex in native languages. Their use may require that one precisely locate oneself, with respect to the person being addressed, with a pronoun in terms of age, status, kinship, sex, and situation. Some names are considered very private because they are so closely identified with a person. Such private names would only be known by the closest relatives and acquaintances and used only in carefully regulated situations. And we must not forget the English names by which Native Americans are identified for official purposes by school and government officials. Even these names distinguish an aspect of the identity of Native American persons, an aspect often not of their choosing.

Practices associated with naming demonstrate the close association between the identity of a person and his or her names; and also suggest the great complexity associated with personality and character. While names distinguish a person among a community, they also help shape and mold a person within the various communities and domains of culture in which he or she must have a place.

The formal practices that are engaged in starting the individual person on his or her road of life have a religious or symbolic character. While these life-beginning moments reflect beliefs about the nature of human existence and introduce the terms of one's destiny, they also create forms for the person, through which he or she may enter—not only into these beliefs, but into the whole way of life with which they are identified. Naming is an important way of giving a person a place upon which to stand.[5]

RELIGIOUS AWARENESS THROUGH DISENCHANTMENT

As Hopi children attain the age of reason, around the ages of seven to ten, their first step into formal participation in the Hopi religious life is taken in their initiation into what has been called "the kachina cult." Prior to their initiation, children are carefully protected from seeing kachina dancers without their masks in place; and from seeing any mask that is not being worn. Much effort is spent to create for the children a firm identity between the figures who appear as kachinas and the kachina spirits. From the children's point of view, the identity is obvious, for they have no basis for distinguishing the costume and mask from the persons wearing them. The uninitiated child's relationship with kachina figures is close and extensive, and children frequently observe kachinas in their villages during more than six months out of every year. They often receive gifts from these powerful and beautiful figures. They are told stories about them, and they recognize them as perfect beings upon whom depends the entire Hopi way of life. Some kachinas have a fearful appearance and threaten misbehaving children, frightening them into more acceptable and Hopi-like behavior. Children often imitate kachina dancing and emulate the high qualities identified with kachinas.

During the process of initiating the children into the kachina cult, the image that the children hold of the kachinas undergoes a severe transformation. The initiation rites occur during February in conjunction with the Powamu ceremony, which is the first major ceremonial in the kachina season. The children are taught many new things about their culture and especially about the origin and nature of kachina spirits. They undergo a ritual whipping, which serves as a reminder of the price they would pay if they revealed the secrets they have been told about the kachinas to the uninitiated. But the greatest effect of the initiation rites comes at the conclusion of Powamu during a dance that occurs in the kivas late at night. The newly initiated children are privileged to attend this dance for the first time. From within the kiva, they hear the Powamu kachinas approach, and they see and hear the kachina father invite them into the kiva to dance. As the dancers descend the ladder into the kiva, the newly initiated children observe that the kachinas are not what they had expected—for in place of the beautiful kachina heads are human heads—and even worse, the children recognize them as their own male relatives. The immediate response of the children is often one of severe disenchantment, for the sudden recognition that the kachinas are masked impersonations threatens all that they have come to associate with the kachina figures. This leaves the Hopi children, at the very threshold of a formal religious life, with serious doubts about the reality of the spiritual figures whom they had believed were essential to the Hopi way of life.

While it is clear that the Hopi consider this disenchantment to be a necessary stage in the religious development of the child, we must be careful not to assume that what the child learns is that kachinas are nothing more than impersonations. On the contrary, what is shown to the Hopi child through this disenchanting experience is that things are not simply what they appear to be; that reality includes much more than what one perceives with the eyes. It places the child in a position to learn what is perhaps the most important lesson in his or her entire religious life: that a spiritual reality is conjoined with, and stands behind, the physical reality. Certainly it is this realization that marks the beginning of religious awareness. For those who cannot comprehend this level of reality, the impersonation of kachinas could never be more than playacting. The experience of disenchantment strikes a deathblow to the naiveté that is characteristic of the uninitiated. The initiates can never return to that perspective again, for they now know what, until now, they could not even imagine. This knowledge establishes an agenda of religious inquiry and a keen interest in pursuing it. The meaning of one's life depends upon it. This process of inducting children through the passage into religious awareness is not unique to the Hopi; it can be found in a variety of forms throughout North America.[6]

INITIATION AT PUBERTY

As the sun begins to rise, a beautifully dressed young Apache girl walks to the dancing ground to take her place on a buckskin in front of a singer and line of drummers. They all face toward the rising sun. She carries a cane crooked at one end and decorated with brightly colored ribbons and feathers. Facing the rising sun, the girl dances to songs that tell the story of Changing Woman, who, by her womanly powers of creativity, gave origin to the world as the Apache know it. As the girl dances, she prays that she might be given the creative powers of Changing Woman, the powers to continue the creation process of the Apache tradition. By the time the set of songs has ended, she has received these powers and in this way is transformed from a girl into a woman. She has acquired the role, the status, and the spiritual power that accompany the beginning of her menstruation, which she has recently experienced. The transformation is completed and celebrated in a four-day ceremony that follows, perhaps the grandest of Western Apache ceremonials. In their language, it is called *na ih es*, which means "preparing her" or "getting her ready"; but it is commonly referred to in English as the Sunrise Dance.[7]

Preparations for the ceremony begin long before it is to be performed. The family sponsoring the ceremony must select and prepare a dance ground with various dwellings and cooking enclosures. Huge amounts of food must be acquired to feed the hundreds of guests who will attend. A medicine man must be found to sing the ceremony; a group of elders must be convened to plan the ceremony and advise the family on the proper procedures; a woman who will serve as model, teacher, and sponsor of the pubescent girl must be found; the ritual paraphernalia and costume must be prepared.

The four days before the ceremony begins are filled with preparations at the ceremonial grounds. Family and friends gather for the intense effort required to make ready. During the evenings of these days of preparation, dances last until around midnight. These are major social occasions, attended by many. They feature "lady's choice" dancing, affording the girls a chance to make contact with eligible boys they admire.

On the day before the ceremony begins, the ritual paraphernalia for the girl is prepared by her male relatives under the direction of the medicine man. All must purify themselves in a sweat lodge before they may engage in this important activity. The social dancing on the last evening before the ceremonial begins is the occasion for the first public appearance of the initiate. She appears in a buckskin dress of a Plains style with her ceremonial paraphernalia. The medicine man sings songs during this dance. The girl dances in a demure manner, in notable contrast to the gaity of the other dancers.

Central to the ceremonial paraphernalia is the cane. It is a crooked staff made of hard wood so that it will not bend or break. It will serve this woman as an aid in walking when she reaches old age. It is decorated in a complex fashion, recalling cosmic orientations as well as factors related to the privileges and responsibilities of Apache womanhood. It is considered an agent of prayer and an instrument of spiritual mediation. The girl is also given a scratching stick, since she must not touch her skin with her hands lest she mar her skin. She is given a tube through which to drink, for she must not touch water directly lest it rain during her ceremonial.

To identify her with Changing Woman, a small pendant of abalone shell is tied to her hair so that it will hang upon her forehead. One of the identities of Changing Woman is White Shell Woman. A pure white eagle feather is tied to her hair—which, the Apache say, will cause her to live until her hair matches its color. Downy feathers are attached to her costume so that she may dance lightly.

On the morning of the first day of the ceremony, the pubescent girl, by means of her identification with Changing Woman and her receipt of the power of Changing Woman, becomes an Apache woman. After this first set of songs, a second set is sung that recalls the event when Changing Woman was impregnated by the sun, a union whose offspring was a major culture hero of the Apache. The initiate identifies herself with Changing Woman during these songs by kneeling and facing the sun with her knees widespread in a symbolic posture of receiving the fertilizing rays of the sun. She sways from side to side with arms outstretched.

The next phase of the ceremony is the molding of the girl, done by her model or sponsor. This woman, selected for her stature as an Apache woman, massages the girl, who lies upon her buckskin. This act gives the girl the form of a woman. Once the massage is complete, the girl runs to the east, encircling her cane that has been erected at a distance, then runs back. She runs to the east four times. Each time her cane is moved farther and farther away. The four runs are said to correspond with the four stages of life.

Four more times the girl runs to encircle her cane and returns; but now her cane has been set in each of the cardinal directions, evoking the cosmic symbolism that appears throughout the ceremonial as number, color, and directional symbols. The girl's running assures her of a long and healthy life.

The four-day ceremony continues in a complex sequence of rituals. It is clear that in these ritual ways, the Apache girl takes on a power as old as the Apache world itself. It is the power at the source of all creation.

Initiate in Apache girls' puberty rite

In her pubescence, she has become a creator; and through this ceremony, she is made a bearer of the Apache tradition of creativity. The
stages and ways of womanhood and life are revealed to her, and she
wins the promise for a long and fruitful life. By virtue of her identification with Changing Woman during the four days of the ceremony, she
has extraordinary creative power. She can cure the ill, she can bring
rain, and many of the ritual acts during the ceremony serve to utilize
this power of Changing Woman for the benefit of the entire community. It is disseminated throughout the community by such acts as

pouring many basketfuls of candy and treats over the girl's head. The symbolic contact with her makes the candy a vehicle for the transfer of power from the girl. The candy is highly sought after and treated as a holy object. Possessing it will assure plenty of food, a good crop of corn—or it may grant a wish.

Much more occurs in the Apache girl's puberty rite than a simple change in the social position and responsibility of a single female. It is far more than a declaration of her availability for marriage. While it is certainly both of these, it is also a time during which the entire Apache community is renewed. The entire world view and way of life, as sanctioned in the stories of divine creation, are reenacted. Changing Woman is made present among the people once again, and through the presence of her power the world is made anew.

Girls' puberty rites are common and widespread in North America west of the Rocky Mountains. We must look at several aspects common to these rites.[8]

Almost without exception, the rites correspond with the onset of menstruation, and they are usually performed for girls on an individual basis. The great differences in attitude about menstruation are clearly reflected in the way these rites are performed. Where menstruation is a condition of potential pollution to men, especially hunters or food producers, the initiate enters a period of isolation at the onset of menstruation. Isolation may last only for the duration of menstruation but is often extended for a period of time, even up to a year. This period is a time for instruction, for self-contemplation, and for preparation to be a woman. The seclusion is commonly ended with a feast or ceremony announcing the accession of the girl to womanhood.

While far fewer in number, some tribes associate the beginning of menstruation with the holy powers of creation, as do the Apache. In this case, her presence brings health, beauty, newness, and a power to cure. Contact with her is sought, yet her potency may inspire a certain fear of her as well.

Among the most universal aspects of girls' puberty rites are the taboos, restrictions, and special observations. These include a wide range of things such as hair styles, dress, posture, demeanor, work, rest, food, and bathing. Notably each of these is accompanied by a statement of what is thereby gained, avoided, or both. So widespread and extensive are these practices that we must take them as serious and essential parts of these initiation rites. If we lightly dismiss them as examples of superstitions or primitive conceptions of cause-and-effect relationships, we will not understand them. They are something like a

metaphorical language, by means of which both desirable and un-
desirable ways and conditions are given expression to the whole community and are firmly fixed, especially to the initiate who must observe
them, by their association with a set of very special actions. They
extend far beyond the personal career of the initiate because they
reflect the extensive degree to which the lives of individual persons are
intertwined with the life of the culture as a whole.

It is notable that rites of initiating boys into manhood are not so
precisely correlated with physiological maturity, perhaps because for
males there is nothing so distinct as menstruation to indicate maturity.
For males, initiation is often linked with accomplishments of food
productivity, with acquisition of a vision, or with the performance of
some extraordinary physical feat. In many parts of North America, this
is true for females as well as males. We will view two of these initiatory
processes in the following sections. We will see that initiatory processes are rarely isolated from community processes; even when there
is an intense focus on the individual, as in the Apache example just
discussed, the entire community is engaged in a life-giving spiritual
process.[9]

THE VISION QUEST

The crushing experience of disenchantment may seem like harsh
treatment for young people. But disenchantment may appear mild
when we consider the widespread practice requiring children to enter
periods of isolation during which they fast in pursuit of a vision
experience. This practice may be confined to the rites of initiation at
puberty; but as we will see, the vision quest often stands at the core of
Native American religious traditions.

In the Great Lakes area Ojibwa culture, it was the practice to begin
very early in a child's life to prepare him or her for a vision fast. The
parents constantly implored their children to engage in short fasts to
prepare them for receiving the power of a *manido*, or spiritual being. By
age eight, a child might fast two meals every other day. Parents might
awaken the child each morning by presenting the choice of eating
bread or charcoal, and punishments for the child who chose bread
encouraged voluntary fasting. While religious awareness through the
visionary experience was certainly momentous, it was not attained
without much training and preparation. During the years of scheduled

fasting, the child was made to think constantly about the power and guidance that he or she would receive in a vision.

The ceremonial fast occurred at puberty. While more attention was given to boys, Ojibwa girls were also expected to do a ceremonial fast at the time of first menstruation. Children were prepared for the ceremonial fast by being instructed on the importance of the event. They were told how to produce a vision and how to recognize and reject an evil vision. Knowledge of the way in which a vision informs one's life was considered essential for experiencing it properly, for the vision would not speak its wisdom wholly at the time it occurred. One had to live one's life according to the vision; and in the process of living, it would reveal its powers through the good fortune, guidance, and protection it would direct toward the visionary.

At the proper time, as judged by an elder, the Ojibwa boy was led deep into the forest, where a lofty red pine tree was selected. In this tree, a platform of woven sticks covered with moss was placed upon a high branch as a bed upon which the youth was to conduct the fast. Perhaps a canopy of branches would be prepared to shelter him from the wind and rain. Left alone in this place, the youth was strictly warned not to take any kind of nourishment or drink. He was to lie quietly day and night on this platform in a patient vigil for his vision. Elders might secretly check on the youth occasionally to give him aid if necessary. If the youth found that he could not endure the fast, he could return home; but he would then have to try again the following year. Further, if a boy had a bad dream or vision, he was instructed to give up his quest and return home to await another year. When visions rewarded the fast, they commonly took the form of a journey into the world of the spirits, a spiritual journey on a cosmic scale. During this journey the visionary was shown the path upon which his life should proceed. He was associated with one or more spirit beings who would serve as his guardians and protectors throughout life. This association was given physical evidence in the revelation of certain objects that the visionary could procure as symbols of his spirit guardians.[10]

For the Ojibwa, religious awareness and the acquisition of spiritual powers come as products of a long, difficult period of preparation. Its significance is great. The process is one of educating children in the ways of their culture. They learn the roles, duties, and privileges of the adults they must soon become. They are shown how essential it is to live under the direction and protection of the *manido* or spirits. The vision quest prepares one physically and mentally to survive a life that may often be difficult. Receipt of a vision serves to establish one as an adult. It is a passageway that must be successfully navigated in order to enter adulthood with prestige and status.

Among many tribes in North America, religious awareness begins in the cultural process that culminates in a vision gained through an isolated fast. But we should not mistakenly limit the vision quest to the birth of religious awareness or to initiation at puberty, for it underlies a religious understanding of reality that is of widespread occurrence in North America. It is an act performed in a wide variety of patterns. In a review of Plains tribes, Ruth Benedict found that the vision quest might be engaged on occasions of mourning, as an instrument of revenge on one's enemies, on account of a vow made in sickness or danger for oneself or one's relatives, on initiation into certain societies, and as a preparation for war. We must also be careful not to identify the vision quest only with the acquisition of what has commonly been termed a "guardian spirit." The whole notion of the guardian spirit is itself very diverse and is usually taken too simplistically; we must carefully review such theological categories that have been utilized to interpret Native American religious practices. Aside from that, however, the vision quest often does not result in the acquisition of a guardian spirit or a spirit of any kind, but rather in the direct acquisition of power. Finally we must point out that the vision quest is not uniform in its procedures throughout North America and is not practiced at all among many tribes. Further, the use and significance to which the vision is put varies enormously.[11]

Even with this great variety, we may still observe what is common to the vision quest: a perception of reality in which the world of spiritual powers is essential to the successful fulfillment of human life. As the culture is given shape and meaning in terms of this fundamental understanding of reality, so too the individual person finds his or her identity, direction, guidance, protection, and destiny in terms of the awareness of this understanding of reality and engagement in it. It is at the core of personhood, joining the individual with a tradition and way of life, often integrating in the process the many domains of human experience and activity, from the banal and physical to the ethereal and mental. Since the vision quest is an individual event within the context of cultural expectations, the uniqueness and creativity of the individual within society is not sacrificed. Each person's uniqueness and creativity is, in fact, not only expressed but obtained through the vision experience and the powers to which it gives access. In some cultures like the Blackfeet, for example, visions may be purchased, an act that gives the owner use of the sacred objects and ritual words, which give access to certain spiritual powers. In this case, the possession of visions is, among other things, a display of wealth.

There are also other matters related to the vision quest. We must consider the distinction between visions and dreams, and we must consider the consistency of the symbolism found in the accounts by which Native Americans describe their vision experiences. There is general agreement that a true vision is distinguished by Native Americans from ordinary nighttime dreams or daydreams. Even the Yuman and Mohave peoples of Southern California and Arizona, whose dreams are central to their religious power and direction, distinguish between dreams of religious importance and ordinary dreams. Religious dreams seem to be of an entirely different nature, and some individuals note that their dreams began even before they were born.

Still, while the vision or dream of extraordinary character has widespread importance in native North America, we must not necessarily deduce that Native Americans are extraordinarily mystical and spiritual, with virtually every person having extensive vision experiences. Certainly we must accept that such experiences are true and do occur; but as interesting, perhaps, is the process that follows the actual vision experience. It is a process by which the abstract, highly symbolic experience is examined, restructured, and ultimately transformed into a repeatable account of the vision experience. Only in the form of the dream story can such experiences be self-consciously used and shared with other members of the culture. In many Native American cultures, there is clearly a belief that the vision experience cannot be immediately understood. In Sioux cultures, for example, the abstract images—or whatever can be described of the content of a vision experience—must be told to the holy men, who may help one understand the meaning of the experience. Here the vision experience is sought annually for four years, and each vision is considered to complement and clarify the experiences previously received. The vision narrative may not be constructed to the point of being told for a long time. Black Elk, whose great vision is so well known to us through his telling of it to John G. Neihardt, did not tell his vision story to anyone for many years. But throughout his life, this story was constantly consulted and doubtless became increasingly clear to Black Elk as he lived his life.[12]

This postvision experience process in no way reduces the importance of the momentous impact of the vision experience itself. Rather it complements it by engaging the processes of contemplation and imagination in constructing a symbolic narrative out of the true vision experience, fitting it into the meaningful context of one's life experiences and the tradition in which one lives—including its oral traditions, rituals, and language of religious symbols.

Seen in this way, we can appreciate how the vision quest simultaneously serves the individual person and the tradition in which he or she lives. We can see how one bears the shape of one's tradition, yet has the opportunity and even the obligation to contribute to the growth and development of that tradition. It is little wonder that the vision quest is such a powerful factor in so many Native American religions.

PILGRIMAGE

When physical geography is invested with cosmic significance, as is so common among Native Americans, physical movement can easily take on major religious significance. Throughout North America exist untold numbers of shrines and physical features that are significant to one or more native cultures. They are significant as world centers, world perimeters, the residences of spirits and gods, the transformed bodies of primordial figures, and doorways to the spiritual world. Some places are destinations of periodic pilgrimages, which enact primordial dramas and serve to maintain the world. Some pilgrimage destinations may lie no farther than a shrine at the edge of the village or field; while others may be many days' journey to the peak of a distant mountain, the shores of a lake, or a shrine in the desert. Let us consider the pattern and significance of pilgrimage by taking a closer look at a particular example, the Papago pilgrimage for salt.[13] This ritual pilgrimage, though not undertaken for many years, remains in the memories of many Papago people.

The pilgrimage destination was the salt beds that form on the beaches in certain north shore areas of the Gulf of California. This destination is located almost directly west of the southern Arizona desert homes of the Papago people. Papago men took the pilgrimage in the summer on an annual basis. A youth might elect to attempt his first pilgrimage at the age of 16 or 17 after many years of training for the arduous conditions he must endure during the pilgrimage. Once having decided to begin making pilgrimages, a man must participate for at least four successive years. Failure to do so might endanger his health. One is classified as a neophyte during the first four pilgrimages. Not until completing 10 or more pilgrimages is a man qualified to be a pilgrimage leader.

Immediate preparation for the pilgrimage involved the preparation of equipment—salt containers, canteens, food, prayer sticks, and corn meal for use as offerings. Many restrictions and procedures were carefully followed throughout the pilgrimage; and many more pertained to neophytes than to the seasoned pilgrims, called "ripe men." A pilgrim must not step off the trail; he must not think of home or women; he must sleep with his head toward the ocean; he must not spill even a drop of water; he must speak slowly in a low voice or not at all. Neophytes must not walk but always run and could eat only two meals a day.

The journey was taken over a seven-day period, carefully routed to lead the pilgrims past water holes and to certain locations for ritual observances. Each stop along the route was the occasion for making offerings of prayer sticks and prayers. The evenings were spent with special ritual orations delivered by the leader to the pilgrims who sat in a circle. These orations told of the significance of the journey and the goodness that would result from its proper completion. Prayers asked for strength to carry out the pilgrimage. The day before they reached the ocean, the pilgrims came to a mountain, up which they ran to gain their first sight of the ocean. Here they made offerings and ritually gestured to bring the power of the ocean toward them. Before they traveled on, they filled their canteens and drank their fill, for the next 24 hours had to be endured without water. Traveling during that night, the pilgrims had to camp close enough to the ocean so that on the following day they could reach the ocean and return to this camp, where they would retrieve their canteens.

The next morning they traveled on to the ocean. Finding the salt deposit about a half-mile from the shore, they ran four times around the salt bed (about one-quarter of a mile long) before gathering the salt. Then they ran the half-mile to the ocean, wading into it with offerings of prayer sticks and corn meal, strewing them upon the first four waves. Having made these offerings, the pilgrims ran along the beach as far as they wanted to go. They could not look back, for once they did they had to turn around and run back. It was during this run that the pilgrims experienced personal visions. These visions, according to the stories told of them, were often associated with things the runner saw, such as birds, shells, seaweed, or the like. Objects associated with the visions were considered to be invested with great power, and they were picked up by the runners. The visions commonly foretold events in the lives of the pilgrims.

After returning to the salt beds, they gathered and loaded the salt, which had dried during the day, on horses to be carried back to the

Papago villages. On their return, they approached the village in the evening, but—as after a war party—they did not enter it. This permitted some of the villagers to come meet them. Young boys came toward them whirling bull-roarers in imitation of the rain the pilgrims were bringing from the ocean. Old women came to collect gifts of salt.

Upon their return, the pilgrims—especially neophytes—were isolated for a period of time while the acquired effects of the great power of the ocean gradually left them, making them safe to engage once again in normal social activities. The pilgrim was isolated during this period in a special enclosure constructed for him. He was given new dishes from which to eat. Every four days, his dishes were "killed" by having holes knocked in their bottoms, and new ones were given him. During this period of isolation, the fathers of eligible girls might approach the parents of the unmarried neophytes to offer their daughters in marriage.

We can see that the pilgrimage is a very complicated ritual process. At one level, it serves as a rite of passage from youth to manhood. This passage is based both on the performance of a feat requiring the strength of a man and the acquisition of supernatural power through contact with the ocean; and on the visions gained during the pilgrimage. It culminates a childhood of physical and spiritual preparation. It initiates manhood and family life.

Yet, as we have seen, religious processes that focus upon the individual person often serve also the life of the entire community. The salt pilgrimage at the grander level is a seeking of life itself. For it is through the pilgrimage to the ocean and the collection of salt that the deity in control of rain is persuaded to release that life-giving substance. The pilgrims bring back not only salt but also rain. Symbolically the pilgrimage draws a parallel between the interrelationship of corn and rain and the interrelationship of salt and the ocean. During the pilgrimage, "salt" is referred to as "corn." This is part of the special ritual language of pilgrims, through which the symbolic associations are established. Hence by going to the ocean, one goes to the source of rain water. Indeed, the rain clouds in late summer come from the gulf to the Papago people, and these clouds denote for the Papago the coming of a new year. By bringing back the salt deposited by the ocean, a substance itself vital to life in the desert, one brings new life in the form of moisture to the Papago world.

This cosmic level of significance in the pilgrimage is expressed beautifully in the many pilgrimage ritual orations. One of the shorter is as follows:

The remains of a cigarette did I place upright.
I put it to my lips,
I smoked.

To the rain house standing in the west I came.
All kinds of mist were bound up there,
And I could not (unbind them).
It was my cigarette smoke.
Circling around it, it entered and unbound them.
I tried to see him, my guardian [lit., "made father"]
But squarely turned away from me he sat.
It was my cigarette smoke.
Circling around, it turned him toward me.

Thus I spoke, to him, my guardian.
"What will happen?
Most wretched lies the earth which you have made.
The trees which you have planted, leafless stand.
The birds you threw into the air,
They perch and do not sing.
The springs of water are gone dry.
The beasts which run upon the earth,
They make no sound."
Thus I said.
"What will befall the earth which you have made?"
Then, thus spake he, my guardian,
"Is this so difficult?
You need but gather and recite the ritual.
Then, knowing all is well,
Go to your homes."

Then back I turned.
Eastward, I saw, the land was sloping laid.
Slowly along I went.
I reached my former sleeping place and laid me down.
Thus, four days did I travel toward the east.
Then in the west a wind arose,
Well knowing whither it should blow.
Up rose a mist and towered toward the sky,
And others stood with it, their tendrils touching.
Then they moved.
Although the earth seemed very wide,
Clear to the edge of it did they go.
Although the north seemed very far,
Clear to the edge of it did they go.

Then to the east they went, and, looking back,
They saw the earth lie beautifully moist and finished.

Then out flew Blue Jay shaman;
Soft feathers he pulled out and let them fall.
The earth was blue (with flowers).
Then out flew Yellow Finch shaman;
Soft feathers he pulled out and let them fall,
Till earth was yellow (with flowers).
Thus was it fair, our year.

Thus should you also think,
All you my kinsmen. [14]

From this example we can see that a pilgrimage is a difficult, even dangerous, journey. The pilgrimage destination is not one frequented or ever seen by anyone other than pilgrims. It is beyond the space perceived by the ordinary person and therefore is a potent or strong place. The extraordinary character of the pilgrimage is marked by such things as special rules and restrictions, special languages, and a ritualized procedure. The climactic moment comes when the destination is gained. The substance of power and the resulting transformations are effected here. Although first an affair of individual persons, the pilgrimage process forms a camaraderie among the pilgrims, a unity and power that is ritually disseminated to the entire community upon their return. The pilgrimage serves to transform the pilgrim as a person in several ways, as from youth to manhood and from religious naiveté to vision-directed maturity. But it also serves to transform the community, even on such a cosmic plane as to effect a new year.

HEALTH AND HEALING

In the Pueblo village of Cochiti near the Rio Grande River in New Mexico, a person who is very ill may ask to be treated by a medicine society. This is usually done when one fears that one's illness is the result of witchcraft.

The medicine society whose help is sought spends four days in its society house preparing for the arduous task that lies ahead. Once the medicine men go to the house of the ill person, the ritual cure builds in a four-day crescendo of events. The sick person is the focus of this affair, during which much singing, praying, and smoking are directed toward his or her recovery. The medicine society must pit its ritual powers against the forces of witchcraft, and the force of this battle and the fear related to the potential consequences builds dramatically. A climax is reached on the fourth night, when the threatening presence of witches is everywhere and it becomes clear that the strengths being mustered by the medicine society must be great enough to overcome the powers of the witches. On the fourth night, a painting is made on the floor with corn meal. Lines of meal are strewn to connect with the doorway of the house. After dark, the medicine men of the society begin to sing as they enter, carrying objects associated with the sources of their healing powers (i.e., figurines of deities and animals). Wearing only a breechcloth and with his face painted, each medicine man proceeds along one of the roads of meal and places his power object upon the meal painting. This meal painting represents the collective medicine powers whose forces are invoked in these ritual procedures.

Into a medicine bowl, water is poured from the six directions sacred to the Cochiti, and each medicine man adds to it some medicinal herbs. Each medicine man then approaches the sick person, rubs his or her body with ashes, and performs an examination. It is actually a process of divination, attempting to locate witch objects in the person's body that have been "shot" there. When these objects are "seen," the medicine men ritually suck them from the body and deposit them in a bowl for all to see.

The curing process also attracts witches, who attempt to win over the sick person from the medicine society and bring harm to the medicine men. Warriors armed with bows and arrows are stationed around the house, but witches may still intrude. They make their terrifying presence known by knocking at the doors and windows and by making their horrid calls in the darkness.

Witches may harm people by means other than shooting objects of witchery into them. They may steal a person's heart, the center of vitality. When the medicine society determines that this is the case, the medicine men have no choice but to attempt a rescue of the heart. They must enter the witches' domain, the darkness of night, and do battle with them in order to recover the stolen heart. Leaving the home of the sick person, the medicine men run into the surrounding darkness with great speed; invested with medicine power, they may even fly. The noises of fierce battle are heard. Sometimes a medicine man returns battered and blood-covered from his combat. Or medicine men may be found tied tightly with wire in a motionless position. But with great effort, the medicine men will overcome a witch and bring it squealing back to the fireside where, in the shadows, it is shot with arrows and killed. The witch is often a small figure in either human or animal form. The stolen heart, in the form of a kernel of corn, is recovered from a bundle of rags. It is given to the sick person to swallow. In this way, the cure is effected; and after sharing food with everyone present, the society of medicine men gathers its paraphernalia and departs.[15]

Witchcraft is but one of the causes of illness recognized by the Cochiti. Some illnesses are attributed to natural causes, and they are treated with herbal medicines and ordinary means of rendering aid, including treatment by scientific medicine in a hospital. A third kind of illness is distinguished because of its tendency to persist. This type, not attributed to witchcraft, is treated by a process that effects initiation into a clan—a clan adoption ceremony. In this way, a person may extend his or her social relationships, an act viewed as a way of procuring good health and guarding against bad health.

Simply from the way in which the Cochiti perceive the nature of health and the processes by which they approach healing and the maintenance of good health, we can see that the conditions of one's body (i.e., one's health) may speak of meanings that transcend a set of physiological, biological, and psychological factors. Health is not perceived as a condition confined to the individual. While in some cases sickness is simply a sign of one or more individual factors, it just as commonly reflects the conditions of a broader social and cultural environment—and even the conditions of the spiritual world (i.e., the conditions that prevail in the Cochiti cosmos).

In the Cochiti view, the cosmos exists because of the precarious balance between the forces of the *shiwana* and of witchcraft and malevolence. *Shiwana* are various deities and spirit beings who serve the world by establishing conditions of fertility, nurturance, and good health. They do not dominate and control the world and therefore must be constantly called upon and engaged in life-giving relationships by Cochiti people. Cosmic order is constantly threatened by the forces of witchcraft, aimed at bringing ill health, bad relations, infertile conditions, and disruptive social relationships. Witches are manifest in many forms such as humans, animals, birds, and even fireballs. In the Cochiti view, the cosmos is a battleground upon which these two forces eternally struggle. Neither can finally dominate more than temporarily.

Witchcraft is a subject that runs throughout many Cochiti oral traditions, attesting the extent to which it influences the entire Cochiti way of life. Clearly it is a constant factor in social relations, in one's attitudes toward oneself and others, in an individual's perception of his or her place in the family, society, and whole Cochiti cosmos.

With only this scant description of the religious thought of the Cochiti as background, we can better understand what is involved in the curing rituals described. We can now see that the medicine society is engaged in nothing short of enacting cosmic processes. It spends much time preparing for and invoking the forces of the *shiwana* through prayers, songs, offerings, the use of figurines, shamanic techniques of divination and witch-object extraction, ritual battles, and a host of symbolic patterns that choreograph and coordinate the many acts into a unified, strongly significant event.

When we encounter such an event, we tend to see it as an event sincerely done by the culture involved; but in our basic doubt that witchcraft exists, we translate the curing process to a combination of terms that fits our more limited sense of health and healing. Clearly this can lead to only a limited understanding, if any at all, of the event. We avoid asking, "Are there *really* witches?" probably because we feel quite sure that there are not. We add to this the knowledge that it is the medicine society that creates the effects of the witches. This allows us to see the affair as a theatrical performance that has certain psychological effects on the sick person.

Seen in the broader religious context, however, we may understand that witch forces are as real as the forces of good health and good social relations. Both are felt by individual persons at Cochiti. It is the certainty of, more than just the belief in, the reality of witches and *shiwana* that shape the individual, the order of social relations, and the Cochiti way of life. In the curing performances, the ritual and symbolic acts of the medicine society serve to focus one's attention upon aspects of both sets of forces; but they go far beyond this, actually evoking the presence of these forces. Clearly, for those present, the forces of witchcraft are felt. We can understand that, for the Cochiti on the occasion of illness, the very fact of illness attests to the reality and presence of the influence of witchcraft.

Further, we may be skeptical of the actual efficacy of the cure of an illness treated in such a way. I see no reason for doubting that the powers and forces evoked in symbolic affairs have accompanying physiological and psychological effects. But when seen in this religious sphere, illness is often more than a physiological condition; it is often even more than a condition of the individual who suffers the symptoms. Therefore we must consider the efficacy of the cure not simply in physiological terms but rather in the terms by which the illness itself is understood. At this point, we can recognize the efficacy of curing rites at many levels—from the transmission of world views, by addressing and evoking the fundamental powers and way of life in the culture, to the repairing of strained social relationships.

Matters of maintaining health are a major part of the religion of many Native American cultures. Yet perhaps because at some levels they appear to conflict so sharply with the practice of Western scientific medicine, these aspects of Native American religions have been greatly misunderstood—or truncated to a consideration of "primitive psychology" or "primitive pharmacopoeia." This matter becomes especially critical when we attempt to understand a Native American religion such as the Navajo, which centers upon health as the basic component of the symbolic language of the religious tradition. Remember the Navajo hero stories in Chapter 1 that tell of the sufferings of the ancestral figures who courageously risked their lives in order to reveal the significance of relations, of limitations, of place? Chapter 2 discussed the performance of prayer acts in Navajo healing rituals, and in Chapter 3 we considered the cure ritual of sandpainting. In the Cochiti and Navajo examples, we see the remarkable degree to which health can be utilized as the core of a highly complex religious tradition. We see how health is concerned with the individual within the culture, for it is motivated by and directly serves the felt needs of the individual; yet matters of health are also the vehicle for the expression and effecting of cosmic processes, giving the most global framework of meaning in which the individual, culture, and tradition find purpose and meaning. Often in Native American cultures, the condition of one's health is the simultaneous barometer of the status or condition of the place on which one stands and the symbolic language used to gauge and express that status or condition. (Recall our discussion of the essential importance of place in understanding one's religiousness in Chapter 1.)

THE JOURNEY'S END

In her beautifully poignant short story "The Man to Send Rain Clouds," the Laguna Pueblo writer Leslie Silko describes the events at the end of the old man Teofilo's life. When his children find him dead at a sheep camp, they paint his face and tie a small feather in his hair. There was a smile on his son's face as he strewed corn meal and pollen in the wind and bade his father to send rain clouds.[16] In even this minor aspect of the funeral rite of passage, the Pueblo belief in the interdependence of the living and the dead is revealed. If one lives a proper life into old age, he will become a cloud or kachina spirit in death. These spiritual entities, then, are identified with the life-giving substance rain. For many cultures in North America, the journey along life's road does not end in death but continues beyond this life and world. In some cultures such as the Pueblo, that afterlife may remain in intimate interrelationship with the world of the living. Hence there is an affinity between the dead and the spiritual world. In other cultures, it is quite the opposite; the dead are identified with potentially malevolent ghosts and witches.

Quite commonly in North America, the language of human destiny, the goal of life, is phrased as living a life of good health leading to a death in old age. Hence death in old age is often not an imbalance in cosmic forces or the final failure of efforts to ward off ill health but a passage that has been prepared for throughout the journey along life's road. With death in advanced age as life's goal, however, a premature death can be understood as a matter for serious concern—since it speaks not only of the plight and destiny of the deceased but of the status of the world in which the person has lived and died. This view is in direct continuity with the view of health, for untimely death is the ultimate condition of illness. It may be considered a time of grave danger, of high suspicion aimed even at members of the family and community, and of self-contemplation by the living about the conditions that led to this death.

Funeral rites are rites of passage, for they resolve the state of impropriety that arises at death: the presence of a dead person in the domain of the living. The rite resolves this condition by inducting the deceased into the domain of the dead. This is a particularly important religious occasion; for whatever the status of the dead, a funeral rite of passage necessarily involves the contact of the two cosmic spheres symbolically associated with the living and the dead. The occasion of death, therefore, affords a religious community the opportunity to address such things as eschatology (i.e., final and ultimate things) and destiny. Because of this religious aspect of funeral and mortuary customs, we may learn something of the religious beliefs of prehistoric peoples from burials. This aspect is not, of course, peculiar to Native America but is a central factor in the general study of religion in prehistoric times.

Death is a major subject in Native American oral traditions. Stories that deal with various aspects of death include the origin of death, visits by mortals to the land of the dead, and the journey by a husband

to the land of the dead in search of his dead wife. This latter story is of
particular interest because of its widespread incidence in North America and its identification with the classical Greek story of Orpheus and Eurydice.[17]

Many examples could be presented to demonstrate the importance of death in the religious life of Native American peoples, but we must at this point be satisfied with calling attention to the extent and complexity of the religious aspects of death. For life's road to be meaningful, it must lead somewhere—it must have a destination. Death is therefore either the event of life's ultimate fulfillment or ultimate failure. Few moments in the life of the individual can rival the moment of death for bearing religious significance.

CONCLUSION

It has become clear in this chapter that many aspects of the religions of Native American peoples are focused upon the individuals in those cultures. We must review the character of the religious aspects of life's road in order to understand it. The word "individual" is commonly used to indicate a person set against society; we often think of individual freedom in terms of the degree to which one stands apart from society, is free of the binding regulations and seeming depersonalizations of society.

After viewing the examples discussed in this chapter, we can state that for many Native Americans this is not the case. While persons are subjects of numerous formal religious events throughout their lives, these religious events serve also to integrate them into society and the traditions that give it common identity and meaning. (It is, perhaps, more fitting to refer to the Native American as "person" rather than "individual," in order to emphasize attributes of identity, character, value, and role—rather than to designate a unit distinct from the collective.) We have seen in our examples that the Native American person is often given identity, nurturance, direction, and motivation in the very process of becoming integrated with society. And we have come to appreciate that, while freedom for Native American persons is definable only in societal terms, this freedom is nonetheless very great.

We have found that Native American roads of life may be seen as a sequence of passages that conduct persons from stage to stage throughout life. But they must also be seen as processes of the introduction and accumulation of knowledge, techniques, responsibilities, privileges, and relationships sanctioned by the religious character that sustains and gives life meaning.

NOTES

1. See Chapter 7 for a discussion of usage and occurrence of the term "pan-Indian."
2. Don Talayesva, *Sun Chief: The Autobiography of a Hopi Indian* (New Haven: Yale University Press, 1942), p. 25.
3. Ruth Bunzel, *Zuni Ritual Poetry*, Smithsonian Institution, Bureau of American Ethnology, 47th Annual Report (Washington, D.C., 1929), p. 635.
4. N. Scott Momaday, *The Names: A Memoir* (New York: Harper & Row, 1976), unnumbered page preceding p. 1.
5. For examples of naming practices, see George A. Pettitt, *Primitive Education in North America* (Berkeley: University of California Press, 1946), pp. 59–74.
6. For further discussion, see Sam D. Gill, "Hopi Kachina Cult Initiation: The Shocking Beginning to the Hopi's Religious Life," *Journal of the American Academy of Religion* XLV2 Supplement (1977): A:447–64.
7. Keith Basso, *The Gift of Changing Woman*, Smithsonian Institution, Bureau of American Ethnology Bulletin no. 196 (Washington, D.C., 1966), pp. 113–73.
8. See Harold E. Driver, *Girls' Puberty Rites in Western North America*, Anthropological Records Series (Berkeley: University of California Press, 1941).
9. See George A. Pettitt, *Primitive Education in North America* (Berkeley: University of California Press, 1946), pp. 40–58, 87–104 for further examples.
10. For descriptions, see Ruth Landis, *The Ojibwa Woman* (New York: Columbia University Press, 1938), pp. 1–16; and for vision stories, see J. G. Kohl, *Kitchi-Gami* (1860; reprint ed., Minneapolis: Ross & Haines, 1956), pp. 204–42.
11. See Ruth F. Benedict, "The Concept of the Guardian Spirit in North America," *American Anthropological Association Memoirs* 29 (1923); and Ruth F. Benedict, "The Vision in Plains Culture," *American Anthropologist* 24 (1922): 1–23.
12. John G. Neihardt, *Black Elk Speaks* (Lincoln: University of Nebraska Press, 1961), pp. 20–47.

13. See Ruth Underhill, *Papago Indian Religion* (New York: Columbia University Press, 1946), pp. 211–42; and Ruth Underhill et al., *Rainhouse and Ocean: Speeches for the Papago Year* (Flagstaff: Museum of Northern Arizona Press, 1979), pp. 37–70.

14. Underhill et al., *Rainhouse and Ocean*, pp. 66–67. Used by permission.

15. See J. Robin Fox, "Witchcraft and Clanship in Cochiti Therapy," in *Magic, Witchcraft & Curing*, ed. John Middleton (Austin: University of Texas Press, 1967), pp. 255–84.

16. Leslie M. Silko, "The Man to Send Rain Clouds," in *The Man to Send Rain Clouds: Contemporary Stories by American Indians*, ed. Kenneth Rosen (New York: Viking, 1974), pp. 3–8.

17. See Åke Hultkrantz, *North American Indian Orpheus Tradition* (Stockholm: The Ethnographical Museum of Sweden, 1957).

CHAPTER 5

Ways of Life

At Hopi in northern Arizona, when the sun reaches a certain place on the horizon in springtime, people gather in their fields some distance from the villages. The men enter a shade (i.e., a partial enclosure) where they smoke and offer prayers. Then after placing prayer sticks on the ground before a shrine at the edge of each field, the leader of the planting party takes a handful of corn meal and sprinkles it about the shrine in the six sacred directions as he prays for rain and good crops.

The planting is performed in a ritually defined manner, with each specified act associated either with the hope of avoiding some disaster or with some encouraged benefit. Planting is but one step in a series of activities that engage the Hopi in an annual cycle. These countless events in total constitute the Hopi way of life, and few of these events do not involve corn in one or another form. Corn is an inextricable part of the Hopi way of life.

The Naskapi of the Labrador peninsula are hunting peoples. In the spring, they go to the dens of bears just before the bears emerge from hibernation. Standing before the den, they address the bear as "grandfather" or "grandmother" and, before striking the fatal blow, they apologize for their need to kill it. They thank it for giving its flesh that they might be sustained in life. After killing the bear, they place tobacco in its mouth and proceed with the butchering and the distribution of meat in a ritually prescribed manner. The bear skull is decorated with paint and mounted on a pole or suspended from a tree where it serves as an important ritual object for the people during the following year. The Naskapi religious beliefs and practices—indeed, their whole way of life—find a language of expression in hunting and in the animals which sustain life.

In spring at the time of catching the first salmon or gathering the first acorns—the foods that most sustained the tribes in northwest California—an extended ceremonial was performed. Although it took a variety of quite complex and extensive forms among the several peoples who lived in that area, it was generally performed for the purpose of making the earth firm, celebrating the first fruits, extinguishing the old fires and kindling a new fire, and preventing disease and calamity in the year to come. In short, these rites, so closely associated with the foods that sustained the people, amounted to a "world renewal," as Alfred Kroeber called them.[1] The way of life, indeed the whole world, was given its center and place of origin in the vital association with the first fruits harvested from the streams and surrounding lands.

Environmental factors have usually been considered as constraints in the study of Native American cultures. People are restricted by the climate and terrain in which they live and by the type and availability of food resources. These ecological factors have been recognized as shaping the development of social relationships, technology, art, and religion. Although we can scarcely argue with these observations, an alternative perspective is more fruitful when considering Native American religions.

As we have already frequently observed, environmental elements, no matter how commonplace or simple, are grasped by Native Americans with an imagination that transforms mere surface appearances into vehicles for expressing and guiding their conceptions of the nature of reality and human existence. The commonplace is given huge significance, often in cosmic proportion.

We would, of course, expect Native Americans to utilize elements of their common sustenance activities in the symbolic language by which they come to terms with each other, with reality, and with the origin, meaning, and destiny of human beings. If one is a hunter living upon the flesh of animals, equipped with tools and sheltered by structures made of animal bones and skins, it is scarcely surprising that the language of religious expression is built around animals' habitats and characteristics, the hunt, and the interrelationship between hunter and hunted. The religious symbols of fishers and farmers likewise reflect their sustenance modes.

If the Native American activities of acquiring and preparing food—

that is, their use of the environment for sustenance—are considered only in simple, pragmatic terms, we will fail to appreciate the degree to which Native Americans creatively and imaginatively use these aspects of life in facing the problems of human existence and in seeking meaning from them. We will also be confounded at the peculiar behavior that accompanies common sustenance activities because it cannot be satisfactorily understood as simply utilitarian. We would then be forced to dismiss this behavior as evidence of primitive fallacies or senseless superstitions. Certainly many religious rites associated with hunting, fishing, and farming may also function to preserve ecological balances—but this is not a wholly sufficient understanding.

In this chapter, we will look at some examples illustrating the relationship between sustenance modes and religion. This discussion will also introduce us to another major form of Native American religious activity and belief.

BEAR CEREMONIALISM

Since human beings first appeared on earth, perhaps 2 million years ago, they have sustained themselves primarily by hunting and gathering. Agriculture was discovered as a possible mode of sustaining human cultures only about 10,000 years ago, and few cultures that in time became agricultural gave up hunting entirely. Scant evidence exists of the religious beliefs and practices of most human beings throughout human prehistory, for that prehistoric evidence must be gleaned from surviving artifacts, which reveal only dim shadows of these early religions. Yet it seems clear that religious expression was closely associated with hunting activities. Caves in Europe have yielded evidence that humans who hunted bears as early as the Upper Paleolithic gave special attention to the treatment of the bones of their game. They placed the leg bones through the cheek arches of the skulls and carefully oriented the skulls in caches in their cave dwellings. While these events occurred geographically far from America, they are nonetheless important because the religious practices of many circumpolar hunting peoples, including those in North America, often center upon the bear and frequently include ritual treatment of the bear carcass and bones. Scholars considering the widespread incidence of bear ceremonialism and its correlation with artifactual evidence datable from very early human times have concluded that bear ceremonialism is perhaps among the oldest forms of religious practice.[2]

Let us consider a more contemporary example. Numerous peoples of the Algonquin stock occupy eastern Canada from the area between the Great Lakes and Hudson Bay eastward through Labrador. Included are the Eastern Cree, numerous bands of Ojibwa, and the Montagnais and Naskapi, as well as the Eskimo to the north. Throughout this area, bears of various kinds were sought as a major source of food. Bear hunting was conducted according to complex religious procedures. While the hunting rites varied in detail from group to group, a fairly representative picture can be drawn from a description of the hunting ceremonials of the Northern Saulteaux, an Ojibwa people.

Among the Northern Saulteaux, the black bear was given most consideration. Treatment of the bear approached the level of veneration. In hunting the bear, special procedures were carefully followed. A hunter would not kill a bear until he had first addressed it, using a specified name or kinship designation. In this address, the hunter would apologize for having to kill the bear, explaining that it was only because of his great hunger and his people's need for food. He would plead with the bear not to become angry, a concern not for the hunter's safety but rather for the continuing presence of bears to provide for the people's needs. The kill was accomplished only with a war club or a knife. Upon killing the bear, the hunter would immediately dress it in fine clothing so that it took on the appearance of a human being. The Saulteaux explanation for this practice is notable. They explain that

> the bears have a king, or chief, and the orders of this chief must be obeyed. Sometimes he orders a bear to go to an Indian trap. When a dead bear is dressed up it is done as an offering or prayer to the chief of the bears to send more of his children to the Indians. If this were not done, the spirit of the bear would be offended and would report the circumstances to the chief of bears who would prevent the careless Indians from catching more.[3]

Beyond this honoring of the bear, the Saulteaux also erected a pole upon which were hung the skull of the bear, the skin of the bear's muzzle, and its ears. Offerings of tobacco and ribbons were hung on the pole. It was ritually prepared and left standing even when the hunters moved on, a means by which the hunters showed respect for the slain bear and for the "chief" or owner of the animal species, thus assuring the continuity of success in hunting.

The butchering was conducted according to ritual prescription, as was the distribution of the flesh. The hunter cut a small piece of the heart to be offered to the spiritual owner of the bear species and

Pole with bear skull, ears, and muzzle

consumed the remainder himself in order to acquire the cunning and courage of the bear. The tongue and heart were not to be eaten by women, and the bones were not given away or left to be eaten by dogs. They were placed on platforms in trees for their protection.

Hunting rituals are also performed for other animals by the Northern Saulteaux and other peoples of this area. At their camp, hunters frequently erected a staff, upon which they displayed the skulls or heads of the animals and birds they pursued.[4]

This abbreviated description of hunting rites raises two interesting topics. First is the treatment of the bear and other animals as though they were persons; and second is the belief in a chief or owner of an animal species. Both are widespread and common among Native American hunting peoples.

It is widely reported that hunting peoples in this and other areas consider bears to be equal in intelligence to humans and capable of understanding everything that is said to them. Numerous are the reports of hunters who talk a bear into one or another action. The language that one uses to address the bear is designed around this belief in its intelligence. We often too quickly accept this way of relating to animals as a typical stereotype of Native Americans, but in doing so we forego the possibility of gaining a deeper understanding of the religious world view that supports it.

A. I. Hallowell, pursuing this matter in the context of Ojibwa culture, has gained an instructive understanding for us.[5] In considering the Ojibwa, Hallowell found that the native category "person" provides a major key to the Ojibwa world view. The category "person" in Western conceptions normally refers only to human beings, but Hallowell found that this restriction does not hold for the Ojibwa. It is a category that extends throughout the material and spiritual world. Still, the Ojibwa are not simply animatists; that is, they do not simply perceive everything in the world as invested with life. Hallowell demonstrated this by recounting the response made by an Ojibwa when asked if *all* rocks are alive. The response was, "No. But *some* are."[6] At the base of the Ojibwa world view is the understanding that anything has the possibility of being perceived and treated on a person-to-person basis. This designation of the category "person" constitutes a basic difference between Ojibwa and European-American views of reality. In order to properly understand hunting rituals, we must consider them in terms of the world view of the people performing these religious activities. The results of such an effort are far different from what we would conclude by translating these practices into a frame of meaning defined by the Western view of the world. By such an effort, furthermore, we may better appreciate the fundamentally religious character of the world view of Native American hunters.

Recalling our description of the Northern Saulteaux approach to hunting, we may now see that a meaningful relationship exists between their perception of the hunting situation and their conduct. When in contact with game animals, the Saulteaux are confronted with animate beings who have the attributes of a bear or other animal but also have the attributes of a person. These attributes are not seen as one inside the other but as aspects of an integral whole. Seen in these terms, the way in which they relate to the bear is sensible.

Hallowell also discussed a related matter germane to our present concern. In his consideration of the Ojibwa understanding of the category "person," he found that a crucial distinction was made between human beings and other-than-human beings. Since this distinction takes shape in the environment of the religious domain, it suggests the distinction we commonly make between natural and supernatural. Hallowell maintains that such a distinction would be misleading because the Ojibwa have little notion of the ordered regularity of movement or of a set of *impersonal* "natural" laws by which the world operates. Causes and effects in the world result from the actions of persons, both human and other-than-human. In the absence of the notion of nature, at least in our scientific sense of the word, the corresponding term "supernatural" does not accurately reflect Ojibwa thought. The common stereotypical notion that Native Americans are peoples "at one" with nature must, in light of this example, be reconsidered and perhaps enriched.

The second issue raised by the Northern Saulteaux example is the belief in a chief or owner of animals. This belief has great antiquity and is found among hunting peoples the world over. Hallowell found that the distinction between human and other-than-human persons correlated in the Ojibwa view with the capability to undergo metamorphosis. Humans are much less capable of undergoing metamorphosis than are other-than-human beings. Life is possible because of the possession of two aspects, one identified with the spiritual soul or eternal life force, the other with the appearances, which are temporal and subject to change either gradually or suddenly, that one may take. These conceptions underlie the belief in the regeneration of animals from season to season and are doubtless associated with the care given to the bones, which are identified with the seat of the animal's vitality. Properly honored and cared for, these bones that represent or symbolize the eternal source of vitality may undergo metamorphosis by regenerating flesh in the endless cycle of reciprocity by which humans and animals interrelate and depend upon one another for life. The conception of the chief or owner of the animal species gives concrete expression to this essential interrelationship between humans and game animals. The Northern Saulteaux envision the owner of the bears as a bear of extraordinary size with remarkable spiritual powers.

Interestingly, these principles also underlie the beliefs about witchcraft and other nefarious activities. The danger of such things is related to the capacity of a malintentioned person to undergo metamorphosis, to change his or her appearance. Widespread are the stories of persons who take on the appearance of bears as the guise in which they pursue their awful deeds. Such persons are known as "bearwalkers."[7]

A central point to reemphasize here is that the commonplace elements of the sustenance activities are not seen simply as food and nourishment but as images of the very nature of reality and human existence. For the Northern Saulteaux, a bear is not simply a large, furry animal that supplies meat, tools, and hide; it is a person with whom one must enter a proper relationship. This relationship is recognized as fundamental to a meaningful life as well as to bodily survival. The basis for this belief is at the core of the religious world view of these hunting peoples.

Given this correspondence between the hunting mode of sustenance and certain ceremonial practices based on fundamental elements of world view, we may be tempted to define a type of religion as "hunter religion." This approach is focused upon a concern for reducing differences and upon constructing general types—but there is more to religion than general types. Surely, even within general types, the differences we may observe are more interesting than similarities. To dismiss the significance of the various ways in which the hunting mode of sustenance is utilized for creative and effective religious expression would be similar to dismissing the difference between a fine furniture maker and a factory laborer who builds crude wooden crates. We may rightly call them both woodworkers, but to be satisfied with that general description dismisses the differences between them and is naive.

We must not be so impressed with surface similarities among the religions of hunting peoples that we dismiss a closer look at the details of those religions. We must appreciate that Native American cultures are scarcely limited in their capacity for developing and adapting the basic terms of a symbolic language of religious expression to fit their existential needs or the specific character of their beliefs.

This capacity can be effectively illustrated by some of the following examples.

THE BLADDER FESTIVAL OF THE ALASKAN ESKIMO

During an intense festival period of the Alaskan Eskimo, the bladders of all the birds and animals slain during the year are inflated, painted, and hung in the men's society house. These odd-shaped balloons are identified with or symbolize the souls of the game animals. The bladder festival, which is well known throughout the Alaskan coastal area, honors these animals and hunters both. At the conclusion of the festival, the bladders are symbolically returned to their place of origin so that they may regenerate and return once again as game to the hunters.

As with those hunters of the eastern and northern regions of North America an entire continent apart, the hunting ideology is associated with the return and regeneration of the game animals. The bladders are treated in a manner similar to the skulls and bones of the bears. But this is to consider only the surface similarities. If we examine any of the Alaskan Eskimo performance descriptions of the bladder festival, we may begin to see the extent to which this festival forms a fabric woven of many community religious concerns.

On Nunivak Island, for example, the bladder festival is performed over a period of many days on an annual basis. It begins with a sweatbath for all the men followed by a dance and a feast, during which the men give their wives valuable gifts. During the following several days of preparation, numerous restrictions and taboos are observed; the women make new clothing for everyone, and the men make new dishes, decorated in patterns commemorating great hunting feats during the year. The men also create new songs, which they all learn for singing later.

On the particular evening when the festival begins, all fires and lights are extinguished. While songs are sung, a shaman performs a symbolic ascent through the skylight of the lodge on a journey to the homes of the animals and their spiritual owners. During this and other journeys, the shaman repairs relationships with the game owners and consults them about the availability of game for the coming hunting season.

Next morning the men are brought new clothes, in which they dress to symbolize the upcoming spring hunting season. As the dishes that the men have carved are collected by costumed messengers, each man sings songs that tell of the feats commemorated in the designs painted on the dishes. These dishes are distributed to the children of the hunters; they will eat from them during the festival. This too stresses the interdependence of food, hunter, hunt, and game.

Once the inflated bladders are hung in the men's ceremonial house, solemnity reigns for a time. The bladders, which symbolize the souls of the game, must not be left unguarded. A fire is kept constantly burning in the house, and no sharp noises or unexpected actions are tolerated for fear of frightening the game associated with the bladders.

The bladders are honored for a period of four days. Every evening during this period, all of the village people gather in the ceremonial house. The men don their wooden hunting hats or animal heads and imitate, in song and dance, the feats of courage they have accomplished during the year. A feast is enjoyed each evening after this performance. On the last night, a shaman enters the sea through a hole cut in the ice. This time he journeys to the spiritual world of the sea animals. Later the shaman reappears at the skylight and tells the people of the events of his journey.

Also on the last night of the bladder festival, five holes are made in the ice in front of the village. A fire is made there as well. After elaborate preparations in the ceremonial house, each hunter takes his own animal bladders outside. The caribou and bird bladders are placed on the fire, and the seal bladders are punctured and placed in the sea through the ice holes. This action symbolizes the return of the souls of the game to their spirit homes. The village people gather by families around the fire and softly sing the sacred hunting songs, which are passed from generation to generation in each family. This singing concludes in the morning, when the men take a sweatbath to remove the taboos and restrictions they have observed. They enjoy a final feast.[8]

Even in this scant description of one bladder festival, we can recognize a wide range of religious factors. It is foremost a rite of the new year. The old year and its activities are commemorated, retold, honored, and set aside with the old clothing, old dishes, and bladders of the slain animals as the new year is instituted. Indeed, the honor paid the bladders presages the coming hunting season, as does the making of new clothing and dishes. The old year is interdependent with the coming year in the same way that the game animals and hunters are interdependent. Looking more carefully at this festival, we can find that the entire social structure, sexual roles, clan organizations, and age levels are given definition and meaning. It is also a period of passage along the life cycle, serving as a time for the initiation of boys into manhood, which is celebrated by their formal entrance into the men's ceremonial house and their first participation in the festival rites. The bladder festival is a major ceremonial not only for the transmission of religious traditions but also for maintaining the structures of meaning within those traditions.

Other Alaskan Eskimo peoples do not elevate the celebration of the bladder festival to such universal proportions.

THE KWAKIUTL WINTER CEREMONIAL

On a winter night, the members of various religious societies of the Kwakiutl people of the Pacific Northwest Coast perform their dances in the Winter Ceremonial lodge. By dancing, members of perhaps the most important religious society, known as *hamatsa*, attempt to lure back to the ceremonial lodge a youth who, some days earlier, was caught and devoured by the great god "Man Eater at the North End of the World." The youth, who is undergoing initiation into the *hamatsa* or devourer society, does not return. At dawn, the members of the *hamatsa* society begin their dance trying to bring back the youth. In the lodge, corpses, skulls, and worms are ever-present symbols of death. As they dance around the fire singing the dance-of-death song, the *hamatsa* utter the cry "hap, hap"—that is, "eat, eat"—in imitation of their tutelary, Man Eater. Suddenly a noise is heard on the roof. As the shingles are torn loose, a wild figure drops to the floor of the lodge. It is the youth, but he has been completely transformed by the Man Eater. He is clothed only in garlands of pine branches with his face blackened and bleeding. The dancers rush at him, but he wrenches free of them and flees through the door.

The dancers quickly erect a pole, which protrudes through the roof of the lodge. It represents Man Eater. A screen with a hole cut in it and painted to represent the mouth of Man Eater is set up in the lodge.

Soon the deranged youth, who has been overcome and transformed into a man eater, returns and climbs up the pole and out of the lodge. Again he enters the lodge through the door, and this time the dancers succeed in catching him; and the whole society engages in the man-eating activities of their tutelary by pantomiming the eating of a human corpse. The deranged initiate, slightly calmed by this, disappears behind the screen by entering the hole representing the mouth of the man-eating god. Again the youth has been devoured. By going to bathe in the sea, the *hamatsa* dancers gradually calm themselves and again attempt to bring back the youth. Through the use of seawater and eagle-down feathers, both of which symbolize wealth and life, the initiate is brought back to be treated further. He emerges through the mouth of the god as if regurgitated. Finally upon crawling four times through a wreath of cedar, which also represents the mouth of Man Eater, the initiate is calmed—or, as the Kwakiutl would say, healed— and thus becomes a member of the *hamatsa* society.[9] This is but one of many ritual scenarios that form part of the Winter Ceremonial.

The Kwakiutl live along the coastal region between Vancouver and Alaska. Numerous tribes speak several languages. Their coastline homeland includes thousands of islands and fjords that bring the sea far inland. The abundant rain nourishes the forest areas enclosing their villages on the landward side. An abundance of food is available through both hunting and fishing. The Kwakiutl are noted for their massive wooden houses constructed along a street bordering the shore and the distinctively carved poles commonly known as "totem poles."

The religious beliefs and ceremonial expressions of the Kwakiutl and other Pacific Northwest Coast tribes are as complex and highly developed as anywhere in North America. Kwakiutl religious traditions are also shaped by concern for the relationship between human beings and the animals upon which they depend for life—though this concern is perhaps not so immediately obvious as in other hunting peoples. The long, spectacular Winter Ceremonial and the practice of potlatching (i.e., the ritual distribution of goods) are essential to the Kwakiutl way of life.

The Kwakiutl year is divided into two periods. Summer, called *basux*, is the time for extensive hunting and fishing activities. The people live in small groups often separated by some distance. This is a time of limited ceremonial activity. Winter is called *tsetseqa*. The villages are occupied once again, and this is the ceremonial time of the year. The Kwakiutl see these seasons almost as opposites, yet as interdependent. During the winter, the entire order of human existence is reversed. The people represent another form of being. They take winter names and corresponding appearances and actions to effect and express this reversal. Winter is the time for return to the primal era when human beings had animal forms, and the people are organized into animal societies corresponding with varieties of spiritual or mythic beings. The winter is actually not a time at all, in the sense of a succession of new moments, but rather a reenactment of that timeless era before and during which creation took place.

In the Kwakiutl view, the universe corresponds with a total community of four parts: human beings, animals, vegetable life, and supernatural beings. Each of these categories has its own hierarchy and sets of antagonistic oppositions, but the four are interdependent and interactive. Essential to our understanding is the interrelationship of human beings and animals. In primordial times, human beings appeared in animal form, a mode of appearance conceived as human beings wearing animal forms like removable masks. Thus human beings and animals were, in primordial times, identical. These humans appearing as animals were also mythic personages and thereby gods. Upon creation, some of these beings removed their animal forms to become the ancestors of human beings, while others retained their animal forms as the ancestors of animal species.

Throughout the summer portion of the year, the relationship between human beings and animals is that of hunter and hunted. The hunter kills and eats the flesh of the animals. Eating of the animal flesh causes the animals to become one with human beings but in human form. It is during the long, elaborate Winter Ceremonial that this relationship is reversed, in order to regain the primordial identity of human and animal in animal form. Human beings take up the masks of animals in ceremonial dances, thus becoming the animals. They return to the original conditions so as to engender the supernatural powers of creation that may benefit the community.

Thus a relationship of reciprocity lies beneath the interdependence of human beings and animals. This reciprocity is completed by the role reversal of hunter and game animal as the seasons change. In summer the animals undergo death. In the winter, by means of the Winter Ceremonial, it is the human beings who descend into darkness and death, thus restoring the animal spirits. In this ceremonial process, human order must often pit its strengths against supernatural antagonists who devour humans. This amounts to a shamanic effort to recover the humans devoured by these deities. The pervasive use of cannibalistic and flesh-eating symbolism appropriately expresses the Kwakiutl recognition of the basic identity of humans and animals. Also expressed in the Winter Ceremonial is the notion of the spiritual counterpart to the physical world. Indeed, the very name for winter attests to this. While the term *tsetseqa* was rendered by Franz Boas, a longtime student of Kwakiutl, as "fraudulent, pretended, to cheat," Irving Goldman's recent analysis of the word indicates that it more conveys the idea of imitation. This meaning corresponds with the Kwakiutl concentration during this time on dramatic masked performances by which they bring to presence, by imitation, a side of reality that would otherwise remain hidden—the spiritual side. For the Kwakiutl, this spiritual side is fundamental.

We see the central theme of the Winter Ceremonial, that of the devouring death and resurgent life, dramatically portrayed in the initiation rites of the *hamatsa* society, part of which has already been described. The initiate to this supernatural order is the son of a member of the society. The rite by which he accepts his inheritance to the society and the shamanic powers it possesses is also the way in which he is introduced to the spiritual side of reality. The youth to be initiated is symbolically devoured by the Man Eater, an antagonistic deity who initially represents death. The Man Eater is depicted as having many mouths all over his body. He has an insatiable appetite for human flesh. He lives at the headwaters of the rivers at the north end of the world, a place of darkness, disease, and violent death. But the devourer is also a source of life, for one who has been devoured is transformed by his identity with the deity. If regurgitated and healed, he possesses new life invested with power.

After the youth is devoured, he is carried off to a remote corner of the forest, a place associated with the house of Man Eater. Here the youth undergoes a vision fast and learns the clan legend under the tutelage of members of the *hamatsa* society. This experience is equated to the metamorphosis of the youth who symbolically resides in the body of Man Eater. The youth under this influence becomes wild and develops a craving for human flesh. He takes a coffin from a tree (the Kwakiutl use this mortuary practice) and prepares and eats the corpse. He must be reclaimed by the society as described.

From this greatly simplified description of the initiation rites of the *hamatsa* society set against a background of the Kwakiutl way of life, we can begin to understand the principles and beliefs that underlie the entire Winter Ceremonial as well as all of Kwakiutl religious thought. We can see that the Kwakiutl hold as vital the interrelationships between hunter and hunted, human and animal, human and spiritual, and summer and winter. Summer is the time when animals are hunted by human beings for the purpose of supplying food for ordinary human sustenance. During this time, animals and human beings appear as they ordinarily do in nature. This aspect of the relationship is reversed in winter, in a reciprocating process that completes their interdependence. Some human beings (the elders or initiated) become animals and thereby represent spiritual beings as they reenter the primordial conditions. The youth are given to antagonistic spirits to undergo death by being devoured and in this way enter a chaotic state of madness. As in a shamanic initiation, the process of mortification and bodily reconstitution invests one with great powers. Thus the youth being initiated into the *hamatsa* society attains shamanic powers and the powers to communicate with the animals. These powers accompany the rights and privileges of impersonating the animal forms in ceremonial dances, which is equivalent to entering the Kwakiutl way of life as ordained "in the beginning" and with gaining a recognized place in Kwakiutl reality.

In ceremonial dance, the spirits are presented in their characteristic forms of movement. The masks and costumes portray their physical forms, and the songs reveal their nature. As in primordial times, all are mythic figures who are human beings appearing in animal forms. To wear a mask is to participate in that reality.[10]

Much has been written about the well-known Kwakiutl and other Pacific Northwest Coast potlatches, in which huge quantities of goods are given away. A recent study by Irving Goldman has reinterpreted this practice in terms that correct and enlighten previous interpretations.[11] Popular views have held that the potlatch is a spontaneous, angry exchange between ambitious rival chiefs, performed in a display of wealth intended to provoke shame in others and establish one's superior status. Goldman shows that if we view this practice narrowly and only in terms of Western views of property, wealth, and rank, we obtain a totally erroneous understanding. These practices may be better understood in the light of the Kwakiutl religious belief and way of life.

The goods exchanged in these ritual proceedings were traditionally animal skins. Blankets and other items have now replaced skins. Animal skins are not considered by the Kwakiutl as merely dead currency; they see them as equivalent to the souls of the slain animals who, by giving up their lives, provide life for the people. The skin, by having visible form, is like a mask because it can be held and passed among members of the community. The animal skins or their equivalent, when ritually circulated among the societies whose work is to make present the mythic order of reality, are thereby participating in the process that is so important to Kwakiutl religion and life; that is, the mediation of the primordial world of human ancestors (animal peoples) and the ordinary world of hunter and hunted. It is through the ritual circulation of goods in which this quality of life is inherent that Kwakiutl reality is integrated and unified. In this way, the reciprocity that binds all interrelationships in the Kwakiutl world is complete.

There are many appropriate times for the potlatch "giveaways,"
especially during the winter and on such occasions as marriage, when
the demonstration of reciprocity is essential. Potlatches are by no
means confined to situations of antagonism; but even when they are,
they serve to complete the circulation of lives and life forces that
integrates Kwakiutl religion and culture into an organic whole. We
may recall that the use of wealth in an antagonistic situation is essential
to initiation into the *hamatsa* society. It was by feeding the maddened
society and its tutelary, Man Eater, with human flesh, with seawater
(symbolic of the wealth of the sea), and with eagle down (symbolic of
the wealth of the air) that Man Eater gave up his hold on the youth and
regurgitated him transformed into a new, powerful being. And it was
by means of receiving goods associated with life that members of the
hamatsa society became calm and effected a cure upon the initiate.

In short, wealth stands for the vitality of the people in the Kwakiutl
view. Through its circulation among the many, sometimes antagonistic quarters of society, it is mediating, integrating, status-bestowing,
and order-defining.

THE WINTUN HESI CEREMONY

The peoples native to the Sacramento Valley in northern California
lived primarily upon the wild fruits that grew abundantly there. Their
chief mode of sustenance was gathering. They did not consider their
abundance of food as simply a product of nature; beliefs about the
sources of food were intricately interwoven with their religious conception of the world. These beliefs required the frequent performance
of ceremonial acts to assure the continuing abundance of wild harvest.

For the Wintun peoples who lived in this area, the most important of
many annual ceremonials was known as Hesi. The date for this
ceremonial was set by a shaman. During a trance, he or she would make
a spiritual visit to the abode of the dead (*bole wilak*) to be instructed by
the spiritual controller of the world (*katit*). The shaman would not only
be instructed about the date for the Hesi performance but also about
the state of the world and human affairs.

The Hesi ceremonial, which lasted four days and nights, was conducted by the shaman in an earth-covered lodge that appeared as a
swell in the landscape. The ceremonial was the occasion for numerous
dances and lengthy ritual orations. Contents of these speeches included stories of the origin of the world as well as reports about

progress toward the earth's final phase of history and the end of the world. A climactic moment during the ceremonial came when the shaman, serving also as director of the entire ceremonial, donned a sacred cloak to become a figure known as *moki*. In early times, the cloak was a garment made of eagle feathers, but by the early part of this century it was made only of burlap strips. This cloaked figure entered the lodge and danced four times around the inside, blowing constantly upon a double whistle before stopping at the rear of the house to deliver a long speech. This was spoken in a high-pitched, squeaky voice with the speaker bowing to the front and sides in gestures emphasizing various parts of the speech. *Moki*, while not a mythic figure, was recognized as a messenger from *katit*, keeper of the abode of the dead. The message from *katit* was mediated by the shaman appearing as *moki*. It instructed ways of proper conduct for the people and encouraged them to follow the Wintun way of life. The message made quite clear that the abundance of food was their reward for proper conduct and for following the instructions of *katit*. *Moki* functioned also to mediate to *katit* the needs of the people during the course of these ritual orations delivered in the earthen ceremonial lodge.[12]

THE ORIGINS OF CORN

The American origin of maize, commonly termed corn, and the great antiquity of corn cultivation in America are fundamental to the history of the cultures of North, Central, and South America. Corn was the most important widely cultivated plant in the New World at the time of European contact—when it was grown in the eastern Plains, and especially the southeastern and southwestern United States—and has remained so among Native Americans ever since.

Probably corn was first domesticated in southern Mexico. In the southern part of Puebla, Mexico, there is evidence of corn cultivation in the valley of Tehuacan dating to 4000 B.C. Corn was developed through the process of domestication from wild maize, which grew throughout southern Mexico; pollen of wild maize can be dated to 80,000 B.C. From its southern Mexican origin, the development and diffusion of corn can be quite clearly traced. Especially helpful in such tracing has been the identification of some 25 developed varieties of corn that can be separately accounted for. The oldest evidence of corn in North America, for example, is a variety of pod popcorn found in the area of Bat Cave,

New Mexico. This corn is datable to 3000 B.C. and can be traced to origins in Mexico. The diffusion of corn cultivation, however, is not a simple story. Some strains can be traced from their origin in Mexico into the American Southwest, then to the Plains areas and on to the eastern United States. Other varieties moved from Mexico to South America through the West Indies to the southeastern United States and finally to the Southwest. Another diffusion pattern emerges from Mexico directly into the southeastern United States and upward along the Mississippi River and its tributaries.[13] Accompanying the diffusion of corn cultivation and other agricultural influences, we may assume, came radical transformations in culture and religion; but the process was long and probably gradual.

Native American accounts of the origin of corn widely (though not unanimously) attribute it to a goddess, a corn woman. In the southeastern United States, a Cherokee story accounts for the origin of both game and corn. Corn woman (*selu*) is married to the master of game (*konati*). Their son finds a playmate, a boy who arose from blood that clotted when raw meat was washed in the river. The blood-clot boy is mischievous and entices his adopted brother into spying on their father when he goes to obtain meat. They observe him removing game from a cave or hole in the ground, its entrance guarded by a rock. After their father leaves, the boys investigate the spot; and when they remove the stone, all of the game flee into the woods and remain fearful of human beings.

The boys also observe their mother producing food by rubbing her body. They believe this to be witchcraft and plot to kill their mother. But she knows their thoughts, and before her death she instructs them in the production of corn. She asks them to clear a piece of ground and drag her bleeding body around over the field seven times. When they do this, corn sprouts wherever the blood of the corn woman moistens the soil.[14]

We may see in this story the vital interrelationship between death and life—between the blood of death and blood as the source of life, a connection so obvious to hunting peoples undergoing transformation into an agricultural perspective. The blood becomes associated with feminine fertility, with waste and elimination, and with soil. The paradox of the identity of life and death is transformed and expanded into the paradox of the identity of waste (i.e., dirt, menstrual elimination, and epidermal waste) and food (corn and other cultivated plants). There is a shift from a tendency toward male domination in hunting cultures to female domination in agricultural cultures, from the sacrificial use of animals to that of humans or deities identified more with human than animal form. We will recall such a ritual enactment in the Pawnee sacrifice to Morning Star as described in Chapter 3.

The stories of the origin of corn take many forms, but they often accommodate other aspects of the way of life. Some Plains stories, for example, link the origin of corn with the origin of buffalo. The symbolism of corn is so profound and pervasive that in many Native American groups, especially in the southwestern Pueblo tribes, to recount the symbolism of corn would be equivalent to a full description and interpretation of the world views and religions of those tribes.[15]

This point can be illustrated by two specific examples. In the eastern United States, among the most common and frequently discussed ceremonial events are the green corn ceremonies, performed annually at the time of the corn harvest. An even richer example is seen in the way of life of the Tewa, an eastern Pueblo people in New Mexico.

THE GREEN CORN CEREMONIES OF THE CREEK

The Creek, along with other tribes in the southeastern United States, were displaced to the Oklahoma territory during the 1830s in that tragic march known as the Trail of Tears. The green corn ceremonies so closely identified with the religions of the eastern and southeastern tribes doubtless underwent many changes, especially during the period of European contact, until their final performances in the late 19th century—though some residual performances persisted after the move to Oklahoma. As a result, the accounts of the green corn ceremonies arise from a wide variety of sources including literate Native Americans, travelers, traders, and ethnographers. These accounts range over a considerable period of time. We can best view the green corn ceremonialism by describing some of the features that seem to be distinctive of these practices as taken from Creek accounts.[16]

The Creek green corn ceremonial is especially well known because of its identification with the term "busk" derived from the Creek *posketa*, which means "fast." The ceremonial occurred in July or August in correspondence with the ripening of the corn. It was performed just when the green corn is at the stage of turning color. Normally the ceremonial lasted four days, but at least one detailed account describes an eight-day variety. The ceremonial activities centered on a square ceremonial ground especially prepared at some distance from the tribe's village or town. Low sheds of log construction were arranged, one on each side of the square and open only on the side facing the square. These housed the various orders of performers. In preparation for the ceremonial, the residences were cleaned out (especially the hearths), friendships were repaired, and trespasses (even crimes, except for the gravest) were forgiven. All fires were extinguished. Four logs, each a couple of yards in length, were cut and placed in the center of the ceremonial ground and oriented to the cardinal directions. In the center, a new fire was ignited by use of a fire drill. Upon this fire the medicine decoctions were prepared, and the men, who confined themselves primarily to the ceremonial ground area for four days, entered a period of fasting, frequently drinking an emetic to aid in their purgation. Food taboos were extended to the whole community. Especially forbidden was the eating of the new corn before the conclusion of the ceremonial. The eating of salt was also forbidden, and relations between the men and women were restricted.

The new fire was known as "breath master," and the medicine men would blow through a tube into the infusion of medicines they prepared on the new fire. Offerings of green corn and other items (including a black drink prepared from roasted green corn) were made to the fire. Later the women were permitted to come to the ceremonial grounds to receive the new fire for use on their own hearths. The men fasted and purged themselves during the ceremonial's first three days, which were also the occasion for a number of prescribed dances by select groups of men, women, or both. On the last day, the fast was broken and the new foods could then be eaten. This was a day of much dancing and mock battles.

From this very general account of green corn ceremonialism, we can see that the ripening of corn was perceived as the dominant feature in the institution of a new year. It was the focus around which life was not only possible but also made meaningful. The busk was a time of peace and forgiveness, of communion and renewal; a time of repair, cleaning, and fresh beginnings; a time for celebrating the forthcoming bounty of life (i.e., corn) in the initiation of a new world; and also a time for spiritual renewal and communion with the spiritual world. It invoked cosmic order through its symbolism and served to originate a new time.

THE TEWA WAY OF LIFE

For the Tewa, as for other Pueblo peoples in the American Southwest, corn is both the primary subsistence and religious symbol. We have already considered numerous aspects of the complex religious systems of the Hopi, Zuni, and Cochiti; now let us turn to the religious system that is inseparable from the Tewa way of life. Work of anthropologist Alfonso Ortiz enables us to penetrate some aspects of this very complex, sophisticated system.[17]

Fundamental to the Tewa annual pattern is the clear distinction made between winter and summer. This is reflected in the social structure that has the summer-winter moiety division; that is, the entire Tewa society is divided into two groups, identified respectively with winter and summer. This distinction was defined at the creation of the Tewa in the primordial underworld known as *Sipofene*, which is located beneath a lake far north of the present Tewa residence. At that time, deities, humans, and animals lived together along with the first mothers of the Tewa—"Blue Corn Woman," who is the summer mother, and "White Corn Maiden," who is the winter mother. From these primal mothers originated the winter and summer moieties. Summer is the time for planting and harvesting corn and other cultivated crops. Winter is the time for nonagricultural activities, especially hunting. Summer is ruled by the chief of the summer moiety, winter by the winter chief.

This dual system seems simple enough, but the Tewa way of life is not simply an oscillation between winter and summer. In the Tewa view, successful progress through the annual and life cycles requires a much more complicated structure that effects movement from moment to moment, the transitions from season to season. This symbolic structure is based upon a process that unifies the natural and material world of the Tewa with the supernatural and spiritual levels of Tewa reality. It is this ordering of the way of life that gives it unity and meaning.

According to Ortiz's study, the Tewa classify all existence into three pairs of linked categories. One aspect or member of each pair is material or natural. In Tewa terms, this single aspect is *seh t'a*, which refers to all existence after emergence generally as "hardened matter"—or literally, "dry food." The other member of each pair is spiritual, either that which never emerged (as the principal deities who remained below the earth surface after the people and animals emerged); or those souls of human beings who, after death, returned to the spiritual domain below the earth surface. The categories are these: Dry Food People and their spiritual counterpart consisting of the souls of their dead, known as Dry Food People Who Are No Longer; Towa é and their spiritual counterpart, known also as Towa é; and Made People and their spiritual counterpart Dry Food Who Never Did Become— that is, those deities who never emerged.

A little more comment may clarify these categories. The Towa é pair serves primarily to mediate between the other linked pairs. In the human sphere, this pair consists of the elected political officials representing both moieties. The Dry Food People are common Tewa people. The Made People are adult Tewa who enter any of eight groups whose primary business is to mediate between the material/natural world and the spiritual/supernatural world. Their efforts assure orderly progress through the annual cycle and thereby assure life for the Tewa people. Generally each of these groups is composed of people from both moieties, both male and female.

The Made People are the religious and social elite of the Tewa, for they control all human activities. Their primary responsibility is to assure the continuity of the processes of life. Throughout the year, the Made People have nine specified periods of activity, called "works" by Ortiz. These are associated with phases in a sequence that must be followed in the Tewa life way. Each of these works engages each of the eight groups of Made People in a prayerful retreat. These retreats last a day and a night, during which the members of the society offer prayers and perform rites to insure that the seasonal changes take place. Each group performs its work separately at four-day intervals, so there is constant activity by the Made People for thirty-two days during each of these nine works.

The works of the Made People effectively create the passage of time for the Tewa. It is in these works that the Tewa world is made to correspond with the paradigm or model established at the creation; and that the natural and supernatural worlds are kept in contact. The human world and Tewa way of life are wholly dependent upon this spiritual world, which "never did become." While these works of the Made People engage both moieties, it is clear when we see the nature of the works that they reflect the basic winter-summer distinction. For example, the work performed in February, which begins just after the Winter Chief transfers responsibility to the Summer Chief, is known as "bringing the buds to life"; that in March as "bringing the leaves to life"; and those in August and September are concerned with harvest. The works of the winter are not concerned with agriculture.

We can see with even greater clarity that these works of the Made People are the basis for the entire Tewa life way when we correlate them with the annual ritual or ceremonial cycle. All public ritual activity on the annual cycle is planned and directed by the Made People. Each of the eight groups of Made People is responsible for at least one major public ritual. Some of these are accomplished by the

Made People themselves in masked performances of the deities who are their spiritual counterparts (Made People Who Never Did Become). Other rituals are performed by the Dry Food People under the administration of the Towa é. In every case, the performance of ritual depends on successful completion of the works of the Made People. The ritual cycle reflects the distinction between winter and summer activities and serves to mediate the effects of the works achieved, by the retreats of the Made People, to the whole Tewa community in public performance. What the Made People accomplish privately now becomes public through these ritual activities.

While all of these works and rituals assure the successful life of the Tewa people, they do not accomplish the mundane planting, harvesting, and hunting activities. But we can see that, by correlating these daily activities with the works and rituals, they correspond with and follow from them. Such ordinary activities proceed only according to this religious mediation and effective action, which assures their proper and successful performance. In these mundane sustenance activities, we again see the distinction between summer and winter activities.

At the base of the Tewa world view is a duality, expressed as winter-summer and material/natural-spiritual/supernatural. This duality is unified and mediated principally by the Tewa system of classifying all existence in terms of three pairs of linked categories. Each of these pairs in itself bridges the material-spiritual duality; and the pairs taken together form a hierarchy that mediates and thereby integrates the winter-summer division, which exists in both the material and spiritual worlds. The entire Tewa way of life proceeds upon the life-giving dynamics of this symbolic organization.

Ortiz's work has also shown us that this same ordering that corresponds with the winter-summer annual cycle is given symbolic form in the Tewa landscape, which is bounded at its outermost limits by four sacred mountains, one in each of the cardinal directions. Each of these mountains is associated with a sacred lake or pond—sacred because beneath each is a group residence of the Dry Food Who Never Did Become. Each mountain and corresponding lake is associated with an appropriate directional color. At the top of each mountain is an earth navel, associated with the spiritual Towa é.

Closer to the Tewa village in each cardinal direction are four flat-topped hills. Each hill has a cave or labyrinth and is the sacred residence of the spirit figures who are impersonated by the human Towa é in ritual.

Still closer to the village stands a major shrine in each of the cardinal directions. This is the residence of the souls of all things which have lived. A final notable set of features approaching the center of the Tewa landscape are the four pueblos or Tewa houses that surround the four dance plazas.

The set of three pairs of linked categories are thus represented by correspondence with these distinctive features in the Tewa landscape. The spiritual/supernatural aspect of each pair corresponds with the outer realms; that is, with the sacred mountains, lakes, hills, and shrines. The corresponding material/natural members of these pairs are represented in the human domain of the pueblos, dance plazas, and divisions in the social structure of the Tewa people.

Further, the winter-summer moiety division is represented in the symbolic landscape, for the north and east are associated with winter, while the south and west are associated with summer. Even the spiritual figures associated with the lakes, mountains, hills, and shrines are grouped within each level of the spiritual hierarchy by their associations with winter and summer. This is represented in the impersonation of these figures, by the costumes, dances, and manners that identify them with the direction and season to which they belong.

It is notable that in this geographic or spatial scheme there is no simple opposition between sacred and profane, between spiritual and material, between other-than-human and human. For example, the earth navels at the extremities of the Tewa landscape mark the dwelling places of the most sacred beings, the Dry Food Who Never Did Become—and are as religiously valued as the "Earth mother earth navel middle place," which is located in the center of the village.

This description of the Tewa religious system may seem complicated, but it only hints at the sophistication of Tewa world views. Beyond suggesting the impressiveness of Tewa religious thought, it shows that, on the one hand, the Tewa make extensive and rigid classifications; while on the other, the interactions of these classifications achieve a dynamic, vital unity that defines a way of life. This way of life is richly meaningful at many different levels in many different ways. Most significant for our concern is that the basis for this complex system is a religious conception of the world, attested by the fundamental truths of the creation stories, by the constant enactment of religious activities, and by the orientation within a sacred landscape. With this in mind, we can begin to appreciate how the Tewa can recognize the cosmic significance of such mundane acts as planting seeds, hunting animals, and engaging in seemingly ordinary social relationships.

CONCLUSION

As we have seen repeatedly throughout this chapter, sustenance—the food upon which life depends—is never seen in simple, mundane terms. It is never isolated as a necessary but otherwise meaningless aspect of life. Food is never seen as simply "for the body." Whether the way of life is hunting, fishing, gathering, or farming, it is inextricably bound with a religious view of the world. It is the spiritual and mythic or primeval aspects of reality that are fundamental to Native American ways of life, this aspect of reality that gives meaning and shape to those ways. It is this religious foundation that makes the killing of a bear, the gathering of herbs and acorns, the cornplanting activities more than simple necessities for feeding the body. This religious foundation makes such activities crucial to the ongoing creation of the world. In such ordinary activities, as we have seen, Native Americans are given a model for a meaningful life as well as a mode through which they may express their understanding of the character of reality; and through which they may express and effect their religious beliefs.

It is most important to recall that while we may be able to recognize certain general religious characteristics of Native American ways of life, we are in no way indicating by this that Native American religions are all fundamentally the same. It seems quite evident that the variety and complexity of religious beliefs, world views, and actions that may be accommodated to these general modes are virtually unlimited. This chapter has briefly presented only some of that diversity and complexity.

NOTES

1. Alfred Kroeber, "World Renewal: A Cult System of Native Northwest California," *University of California Anthropological Records*, vol. 13, no. 1 (1949).
2. A. Irving Hallowell, "Bear Ceremonialism in the Northern Hemisphere," *American Anthropologist* 28 (1926): 1–175.

3. Alanson Skinner, *Notes on the Eastern Cree and Northern Saulteaux*,
    Anthropological Papers, vol. 9, part 1 (New York: American
    Museum of Natural History, 1911), p. 162.

4. See Ibid., pp. 68–76, 162–64.

5. A. Irving Hallowell, "Ojibwa Ontology, Behavior, and World
    View," in *Culture in History: Essays in Honor of Paul Radin*, ed.
    Stanley Diamond (New York: Columbia University Press, 1960),
    pp. 19–52.

6. Ibid., p. 24.

7. See Richard M. Dorson, *Bloodstoppers and Bearwalkers* (Cambridge:
    Harvard University Press, 1952).

8. Margaret Lantis, *Alaskan Eskimo Ceremonialism*, Monographs of the
    American Ethnological Society, no. 11 (Seattle: University of
    Washington Press, 1947).

9. This description is based on Werner Müller, "North America," in
    Pre-Columbian American Religions, ed. Walter Krickeberg (London:
    Weidenfeld & Nicolson, 1968), pp. 209–20; and Irving Goldman,
    The Mouth of Heaven: An Introduction to Kwakiutl Religious Thought
    (New York: John Wiley, 1975), pp. 86–97.

10. See Goldman, *The Mouth of Heaven*, pp. 86–121, for a discussion of
    the Winter Ceremonial.

11. See Ibid., pp. 122–76.

12. S. A. Barrett, "The Wintun Hesi Ceremony," *University of Califor-
    nia Publications in American Archaeology and Ethnology*, vol. 14, no. 4
    (Berkeley: University of California Press, 1919), pp. 438–88.

13. See Harold E. Driver, *Indians of North America*, rev. ed. (Chicago:
    University of Chicago Press, 1969), pp. 66–70, Map 7.

14. James Mooney, *Myths of the Cherokee*, Smithsonian Institution,
    Bureau of American Ethnology, 19th Annual Report (Washington,
    D.C., 1900), pp. 242–49; and James Mooney, "Myths of the
    Cherokee," *Journal of American Folklore* 1 (1888): 98–106.

15. See Gudmund Hatt, "The Corn Mother in America and in In-
    donesia," *Anthropos* 46 (1951): 853–911.

16. John Witthoft, *Green Corn Ceremonialism in the Eastern Woodlands*,
    Occasional Contributions from the Museum of Anthropology of
    the University of Michigan (Ann Arbor, 1949); see especially the
    section on Creek, pp. 52–70.

17. Alfonso Ortiz, *The Tewa World: Space, Time, Being & Becoming in a
    Pueblo Society* (Chicago: University of Chicago Press, 1969).

CHAPTER 6

Tradition and Change in Native American Religions

Among the most sacred and beautiful Navajo poems are the horse songs.

> Its feet are made of mirage.
> Its gait was a rainbow.
> Its bridle of sun strings.
> Its heart was made of red stone.
> Its intestines were made of water of all kinds.
> Its tail of black rain.
> Its mane was a cloud with a little rain.
> Distant lightning composed its ears.
> A big spreading twinkling star formed its eye and striped its face.
> Its lower legs were white.
> At night beads formed its lips.
> White shell formed its teeth.
> A black flute was put into its mouth for a trumpet.
> Its belly was made of dawn, one side white, one side black.[1]

The horse is the primordial form, expressing the shape of the Navajo cosmos. The history and present status of the Navajo people have been greatly influenced by the horse. Even though pickup trucks have now replaced the horse for transportation, horses are still kept by many Navajo families as an expression of their wealth and status. The pickup truck can also be seen as an extension of the horse in the sense that it provides a means of movement by which the people may continue their way of life—a way defined by that paradox of choosing to occupy vast regions of land while restlessly, even aggressively, seeking mastery over distance.

In historical perspective, we must remember that the horse, now an image of cosmic proportion for the Navajo, was introduced to North America by the Spanish only four centuries ago. This raises for us certain fundamental questions not only with regard to the Navajo but to our entire consideration of Native American religions. For this image, which we recognize as so traditional for Navajos, is actually a product of the same European influences so often identified as threatening the very existence of Native American cultures.

A review of the features we consider most traditional, typical, and distinctive of Native American religions reminds us that commonly entwined within their histories are many elements of outside influence, originating both in Europe and in other native cultures. Once we become aware of the importance of historical processes in Native American traditions, we must recognize that we introduce inaccuracies when we investigate Native American religions without taking their histories into account. Every aspect of Native American religions that we have considered has had a place in a long, complex history; and every form of expression and religious act is part of a history. While it has been impractical to give more than occasional reminders of this fact in previous chapters, we must "center in" on these historical processes in this chapter because they are as important and distinctive as any other dimension of Native American religions.

Long, persistent efforts have been made to suppress, alter, and eliminate Native American traditions. They have been forcibly subjected to radical transformations in nearly every domain of culture. Yet many of these traditions have survived by a skillful management of historical events that has permitted them to protect and strengthen their traditions as well as adapt to the changes forced upon them. In light of the actual survival of these traditions under such severe conditions, we must be persuaded that historical processes are among the most distinctively important aspects of Native American religious traditions.

The history of Native American religions is extremely complex and difficult to piece together because the short span of recorded history prevents us from detailing the long story. Even in the historical period coincident with the period of European contact, there has been little concern with recording the religious histories of native cultures. What history exists is, in almost all cases, limited to European interests in native cultures. Thus the known and recorded history of Native American religions is linked directly to the eradication of native "superstitions" and to the Christianization of the "Indians." Our efforts are further confounded by the great number of native cultures.

Our concern will center on the processes of historical development that have variously shaped Native American religious traditions, although our data must be limited primarily to the period of European contact. We will view the processes by which tradition and cultural identity are maintained while being confronted by threatening influences; we will try to discover what role religion plays in these processes as well as how religion is affected by the changes that occur.

Let us briefly look at the histories of three cultures as examples. While these examples do not exhaust the various types of historical processes that might be more generally defined, they do illustrate a diversity of religious historical processes as well as several important new and emergent forms of Native American religions.

RIO GRANDE PUEBLOS

From a tourist turnout on Interstate 40 west of Albuquerque, New Mexico, one can see the Pueblo village of Laguna. The houses of the village span the southeast side of a small hill. Pueblo houses randomly dot the hillside, but the sight is dominated by the Catholic church that stands near the hilltop, easily identifiable by its massive size in contrast to the small houses and by its cross-topped steeple.

One early spring morning, I observed Laguna from a different perspective. My family and I ventured off the highway and drove into the village to visit. Even from this perspective, the Catholic church was dominant, for the people from the village were making their way to the church for celebration of mass. It was a minor fiesta day in Laguna, a gala event with concession stands selling food and numerous visitors from other pueblos arriving throughout the morning. In the afternoon of this chilly, windy day, we went to the village plaza to watch the Laguna dances, but the plaza was deserted. As we awaited the appearance of the dancers, we began to hear the beat of drums, the shake of rattles, and voices singing the Laguna songs. The sounds that came to us on the wind led us to the Catholic church, where we watched the Laguna dances inside. The dancers, both men and women, wore European-American clothing, but some wore moccasins and others wore brightly colored scarves as headbands. All carried rattles as two parallel files performed a native dance step. The priest of the church in his rope-sashed brown robe appeared at the front apparently performing ordinary custodial duties. He seemed to pay little attention to the Pueblo activities that occupied the church.[2]

From the door at the rear of the church, I looked past the dancers to view the Christian symbols—the altar, crucifix, stations of the cross—but some architectural features, numerous designs painted on the beams, and other items were distinctively Pueblo. I thought of the Catholic mission church at the Pueblo village of Zuni, where larger-than-life paintings of *koko* (*kachina*) figures dominate the walls. I thought of the numerous Pueblo villages that cluster along the Rio Grande River, villages in which the mission church is the dominant architectural structure. I thought of the large dance plazas adjacent to these churches, where Pueblo dances, highly religious in character, are frequently performed. These observations of common features reflect certain peculiar anomalies as witness to the present moment in a long, remarkable religious history. It is a history in which Christian and native religions have been in almost continuous contact for 400 years. The first Franciscan missionaries attempted to establish themselves among the Pueblo people nearly 40 years before the Mayflower sailed in 1620; the city of Santa Fe, which lies amidst the Rio Grande Pueblo area, became the provincial capital of New Mexico in 1610.

Most remarkable is that after this long history, the Pueblo people have maintained their native religious tradition and way of life; indeed, our usual image of the Pueblo peoples closely associates them with the idea of an ancient, strongly indigenous tradition. Yet it is nonetheless obvious that the Pueblo peoples (the Hopi far to the west somewhat excepted) have also accepted Christianity and incorporated it into their Pueblo way of life. The tenacity, adaptability, and ability to compartmentalize are all characteristics of Pueblo religious historical processes, which cannot be understood or appreciated apart from at least an outline of Pueblo religious and cultural history.[3]

Based upon linguistic and archaeological data and the projections that can be made upon the ethnographic record, we can indicate the outlines of the prehistoric period that preceded Coronado's entrance into the Rio Grande area in 1540. The peoples who lived in the area during this time can definitely be identified as comprising two distinct traditions that had entered the area at different times. Probably first to enter were the Tanoans, believed to have come from what is now the northeastern corner of Arizona and the northwestern corner of New Mexico. They came from the areas known as Anasazi, Mesa Verde, and

Chaco, probably entering the Rio Grande area between 1100 and 1200. They were followed by the Keresan peoples, believed to have come from the area of today's east-central Arizona. These groups had many differences; their descendants have remained linguistically distinct, and they continue to bear basic cultural differences.

During this early period, these groups established themselves in settlements along the Rio Grande River and its tributaries and turned to an agricultural subsistence pattern adapted to the ready water supply from the river. Their former agricultural methods had depended more on rainfall, but in this new environment they could utilize irrigation methods. Close community organization was necessary to build and maintain the irrigation system.

There is evidence that contact among these two traditions was widespread during this prehistoric period, but there is also considerable indication that these cultures also had much contact with many other cultures. Certainly there was contact with the Apachean peoples who were entering the area from their former homelands in the distant western Canadian areas. There is also evidence of widespread contact with the Plains cultures who, at this time, were sedentary agriculturalists. Thus it seems clear that, during the several centuries before the initial European contact, the peoples living in the Rio Grande valley experienced frequent cultural interaction doubtless accompanied by much borrowing and extensive cultural innovation.

The Pueblo ceremonial system was well developed; and while there were basic differences in approach and emphasis, both the Tanoan and Keresan traditions held as major concerns the control of weather, curing the ill and the maintenance of good health, warfare, and the control of game animals and fowl. Based on projections from emphases that remain distinct today, the Tanoan approach emphasized "works," in the manner we will recall from our Chapter 5 discussion of the Tewa; while the Keresan approach emphasized "magical" practices to accomplish these concerns.

History in its written form began for the Rio Grande Pueblo peoples in 1540 with the appearance of Coronado, who was accompanied by five missionaries, several hundred armed horsemen, and a group of native servants from Mexico. The first encounter was not a happy one for the Pueblo peoples, for Coronado demanded much from them during his two-year stay in the area. Attempts to protest were answered by executions, which numbered in the hundreds.

Second and third Spanish expeditions followed some 40 years later. The second was short, but two missionaries were left behind, and it is

145
*Tradition and
Change in
Native
American
Religions*

believed that they were soon killed by the Pueblos. The third expedition, led by Espejo in 1582, inspired much interest in colonization of the area. In 1598, Juan de Oñate established the first colony in the province of New Mexico near San Juan. For the next century, the Pueblo peoples would be constantly confronted by a complex, demanding Spanish presence. The major arenas of contact were in the Pueblo villages, with the intrusive establishment of Franciscan missions; and in the Spanish settlements, where Pueblo peoples were forced to work for the colonial governors and settlers.

The character of the mission effort is important for our understanding. Franciscan policy frequently rotated their missionaries from station to station and back and forth between Mexico and these northern posts. Consequently the Franciscans took little interest in making enduring associations with the Pueblo peoples. With rare exception, the missionaries did not learn their languages, engage in translating Christian scripture or beliefs into the language, or adapt their efforts to suit Pueblo culture. Instead they primarily exerted themselves to accomplish several goals, each of which they approached in a manner that bred only antagonism and distrust between themselves and the native peoples.

A major concern of the missionaries, which is still in evidence, was an enormous building program. Large chapels and mission compounds were built in the villages by forced Pueblo labor. The size of these buildings testifies to the measure of labor that was invested. The huge timbers that supported their roofs often had to be cut and hauled by the Pueblo peoples from a distance of 20 to 30 miles. By 1630, it was reported that 90 chapels existed in as many villages. The missionaries introduced Christianity in a manner similar to the way they built their chapels. Under punishment of whipping, they forced the native peoples to be baptized, to attend mass, and to make confession. They physically discouraged the performance of native religious practices. Many were the occasions when native religious leaders were hanged as witches and when kivas (i.e., religious chambers) were raided for the ceremonial paraphernalia and masks, which were collected and burned. Missionaries, like the colonists, also forced the native peoples to tend their gardens and domestic animals and to perform other sorts of personal services. The effect was to force the practice of Pueblo religion underground; to introduce a participation in Christian acts but with little internalized meaning; and to breed a deep resentment against the Spanish, including the Christian church.

The colonial arena of contact was no more pleasant. It was a period of encroachment on Pueblo lands. While enslavement was illegal, a system of *encomienda* was established that gave colonists control of the native peoples on the land granted to them. This permitted colonists to force the Pueblo peoples to work for them without compensation.

The supremacy of the Spanish, fully realized by the Pueblo peoples, fostered a resurgence of loyalty and dedication to traditional ways. This resurgence of identity, encouraged by ever-increasing bewilderment and resentment, set the scene for a Pueblo revolt throughout the area in 1680. Carefully planned by a Pueblo man from San Juan by the name of Popé, who had been one of 47 religious leaders punished by the Spanish authorities in 1675, the revolt effectively removed the Spanish from the entire Rio Grande area. Of the missionaries, 21 of 33—and nearly 400 of some 2,500 colonists—were killed; the rest fled to the El Paso area. The missions were destroyed together with all their records and furnishings, and the Pueblo peoples lived free of Spanish influence until De Varga arrived to reconquer the area in 1693. At this time, many Pueblo peoples fled from the area to live among the Pueblo peoples to the west and even among non-Pueblo peoples like the Navajo and Apache. The village of Laguna was founded to the west of the Rio Grande in an attempt to avoid Spanish domination. During that century, epidemics, violent deaths, and dispersal had greatly declined the Rio Grande Pueblo population.

The changes that occurred during the 17th century were enormous but surprising in character. While not forced to do so, the Pueblo peoples effected a wide range of changes in their culture. By 1700 they had added wheat, melons, apples, peaches, apricots, pears, tomatoes, and chiles to their crops. They had acquired chickens, goats, and sheep as domestic animals, adding not only to their diet but introducing craft items made from wool. They had begun to utilize mules, horses, and donkeys for transportation and for assistance with their labor. These additions greatly revolutionized their cultures and have been so totally incorporated that we now identify them with the traditional ways of the culture.

But while the Catholic chapels had by this time come to dominate the village architecture, the Catholic missions apparently had little effect on the Pueblo religious beliefs and practices, apart from forcing performance of the native tradition into secrecy and forcing the tacit public performance of Christian acts. More extensive effects on Pueblo religion resulted from contact with the native peoples brought from Mexico and increased contact among native peoples in the Rio Grande area.

During the 17th century, Spanish had become well established as a second language, providing a lingua franca among the many native peoples whose languages were unintelligible to one another; yet they retained their own languages and even made efforts to keep them free of Spanish words. Spanish became an instrument used by the Pueblo peoples against Spanish intrusions, in that it permitted them to better communicate among themselves. It helped support the growing sense of unity and common identity that replaced the antagonisms that existed prior to Spanish contact.

147
*Tradition and
Change in
Native
American
Religions*

While the 18th and 19th centuries also witnessed major changes in the Rio Grande area, these changes were in many respects less threatening to the Pueblo peoples than those that had occurred in the 17th century. Spanish attitudes and policies changed after reconquest to emphasize colonization, and efforts to Christianize the Pueblos were relaxed. As colonization progressed, the frequent raids by non-Pueblo native peoples harassed colonists and Pueblo peoples alike, and they joined together in an effort to combat these threats. The influx of colonists provided another major charge for the Franciscan missionaries in serving these growing communities.

The 18th-century relations between Pueblo and Spanish peoples could be characterized as generally friendly, both parties being occupied with maintaining their own ways and identities. The thorn for the Pueblo peoples that remained was the Spanish clergy, who continued, though with less vigor, to force participation of the Pueblo peoples in activities of the Catholic missions and to infringe upon them for labor and other services. During this century, the Pueblo peoples apparently perfected ways of accommodating the demands of the Spanish and especially the missionaries by yielding to the performance of certain acts with little or no commitment or internalization of their European meanings, while retrenching and deepening their commitment to their own ways. When borrowing did occur, it was usually accomplished in direct continuity with the Pueblo tradition.

The 19th century saw the appearance of Anglo-Americans and the U.S. government in the area. The largest cultural group was Hispanic; and since these people were most concerned with continuing to establish themselves in the area, they had little interest in changing Pueblo life. New Mexico became a U.S. territory in 1850, however, and this new government influence only added to the confusion about land rights among the several peoples in the area. This period was most difficult for the Pueblo peoples because their legal status with respect to their ownership of lands was in general dispute. By 1881, railroads had penetrated the area, and with them came a new economic base for the Pueblo peoples. A flood of tourists who were curious about "Indians" began to wash over the area. Their eagerness to buy from the Native Americans contributed to the introduction of a cash economy to the Pueblos. (In one report from this period, a Pueblo woman expressed how odd these Americans were, for one of them had bought the stone that covered her chimney.)

Despite all of the innovations accepted in terms of material culture by 1700, the tradition of the Pueblo peoples had remained firm through the two following centuries. The village locations, social order, value system, and ceremonial system had remained in good health. The Pueblos had continued to be tightly integrated, self-sustaining communities living full ceremonial lives. By 1900, several of the mission churches had fallen into ruins, but the Pueblo religious tradition continued to be vigorously practiced, yet with intense secrecy.

With the rapid rise of the Anglo-American influence in New Mexico, the first half of the 20th century was a period when changes occurred on an order far more profound than the Pueblos had undergone in the previous three centuries of contact. Prior to the Anglo-American dominance, the Pueblo cultures had been challenged largely by the Spanish Catholic missionaries who had attempted to destroy the traditional Pueblo religion and introduce Christianity. This effort backfired and resulted in a deeply entrenched Pueblo religious tradition protected by the range of isolating protective mechanisms that had been carefully developed over centuries. Yet the Pueblo peoples had readily accepted innovations in material culture and had established them firmly in continuity with their traditions. These innovations were of a type that permitted the closely integrated, separate identity of each Pueblo community.

But with the Anglo-American dominance came basic economic changes: the introduction of the credit system by establishing trading posts, and expansion of a cash economy. These economic conditions fostered sweeping changes in the character of Pueblo society. In the 1930s, the U.S. Bureau of Indian Affairs engaged in a construction program aimed at bringing Native Americans into fuller participation in a complex economy. This tendency was further expanded during World War II; not only were many Pueblo people engaged in the armed services, but jobs could be easily obtained outside the Pueblo villages. This broad-scale participation in a complex cash economy, once accepted, has continued to expand. Today, most Pueblo communities continue to farm and maintain some semblance of a subsistence-type economy, but this is almost a token effort. Most Pueblos depend on wage and salary incomes from outside the community, often in major urban centers. This has engaged the Pueblo peoples not only in broader interaction and interdependence with non-Pueblo peoples; it has introduced to them the importance of a pan-tribal identity. They have come to interact and identify more completely with other native peoples, a development evidenced by their participation in numerous intertribal affairs and also in the activities of major urban centers that contain a significant Native American population.

The ceremonial system and the practice of traditional Pueblo religion have undergone and survived one of their greatest challenges during this period. The official position of the Bureau of Indian Affairs before 1928 was openly antagonistic toward "Indian ceremonials." It outlawed them and made every effort to discourage the continuity of such traditions, attempting to bring the Pueblo communities into complete assimilation with the Anglo-American majority culture. The Pueblo peoples had well-developed and well-practiced mechanisms to meet this challenge and to renew dedication to their religious traditions. These methods helped encourage a unified resistance among the members of the Pueblo communities.

When John Collier became head of the Bureau of Indian Affairs, he soon changed this position. He respected the traditions of Native Americans and supported the practice of their ceremonials. He encouraged programs to support the survival of Native American communities by helping to establish them in the vital areas of economy, education, and health services.

The result was a series of developments that have greatly transformed the Pueblo communities since the beginning of the century. Today, while most Pueblo villages have survived, the compact village structure has given way to isolated single-family dwellings, often built in new settlement areas. These houses are patterned on American suburban homes with garages, lawns, electricity, plumbing, and all of the furnishings one would find in the average Anglo-America home. Cars and pickup trucks are essential in connecting the communities with job locations and with the external sources of food and other items purchased on credit or for cash. Television has replaced, to a major extent, the sessions of storytelling. Dress and hair styles are largely Anglo, yet still serve to indicate the degree to which a person is "traditional" or "progressive." English has become the second language, replacing Spanish, and with each generation increasingly becomes the primary, often the only, language known.

Broadening of the Pueblo subsistence and economic base has brought greater possibility for the people to internalize the traditional meanings of Christianity and to recognize that it serves the same general needs as the traditional Pueblo religious practices: the health and well-being of all humanity. Still, the ceremonial organization and practice of traditional religion have been retained to a remarkable degree, even though finding sufficient numbers of people to fill the necessary societies and religious offices has become increasingly difficult for many villages. In this area of culture, however, lies the future continuity of identity and tradition for the Pueblo communities.

On fiesta day in Laguna, what I observed was the present phase in a complex, lengthy religious history. Against the outline of this history, we can more readily understand the clear sense of separateness of the Catholic and native practices; yet we can also appreciate the genuine meaningfulness of both these forms of religious practice for contemporary Pueblo peoples. While the separate performance attests to the remarkable persistence and self-preservation of the Pueblo traditions, the voluntary participation in Christian practices and the adjustment of native practices to correlate with the Christian liturgical calendar attests to the present most remarkable stage in Pueblo religious history. It indicates the extent to which Pueblo peoples can extend their ideas about religion to encompass even the Christian beliefs they have carefully isolated for centuries in their continuing efforts to meet the new needs of their rapidly changing cultures.

YAQUI

On the south side of the Phoenix area, just three miles from my Arizona home, is the Yaqui community of Guadalupe. Each year during Easter week, I go to Guadalupe to observe the celebration of their highest ceremonial occasion. The Yaqui church at Guadalupe stands beside the Spanish Catholic church, facing east and overlooking a large, barren plaza area. During Easter week, this plaza area is remarkably transformed. On the side in front of the Spanish Catholic church, a carnival is set up complete with ferris wheel, tilt-a-whirl, merry-go-round, and game booths with their barkers. In front of the Yaqui church, the plaza area is roped off and reserved for the dramatic performances of the Easter pageantry. This area is surrounded by temporary stands, erected by the Yaqui people, in which they prepare and sell a variety of food and craft items to the many people who come to observe the events.

The Easter Festival engages the Yaqui community throughout the period of Lent; but many in the community are totally immersed in the dramatic activities that unfold during Holy Week. At this time, the story of the crucifixion and resurrection of Jesus is enacted as the basic struggle between good and evil. These forces are presented by groups or societies of Yaqui performers.

The Fariseo society is in charge of the Easter ceremonies. In the Easter pageant, this society provides several groups of performers. The "Soldiers of Rome" are a small group whose members wear ordinary dress but serve as officers to the other Fariseo performers. It is their responsibility to direct the fiesta, and they must remember every detail of the extensive performance.

The Pilatos, who represent Pontius Pilate, are the ritual heads of the Fariseo society. They wear black shirts and wide-brimmed hats, and they carry spears. The largest group of Fariseos are the Chapayekas, who are masked figures. Several types of masks may be worn, but the most characteristic is distinctive for its big, flat ears and sharp nose; indeed, the word Chapayeka is derived from Yaqui words meaning "sharp" and "nose." These masks may serve as caricatures of all sorts of figures associated with evil. The Chapayeka performer always carries the cross of his rosary in his mouth to protect him from the evil he serves to manifest. Chapayekas wear an overcoat or a blanket wrapped around them like a coat, with a belt of rattles. They also carry a wooden sword and dagger.

Another group, not a part of the Fariseo society but associated with them in the Passion performance, is the Caballeros. They march with the Fariseos and try to keep the Chapayekas from going too far in their threatening antics.

On the side opposing the Fariseos is the society of the Matachinis. This society presides over all other ceremonials performed during the year. As a group of male dancers, they appear wearing no special costume other than a headdress made of crepe paper strips wrapped around a bamboo frame. They carry a brightly colored gourd in one hand and a brightly colored feather wand in the other. Several other groups also perform during the Easter pageant: the Maestros (teachers), who read the services and serve as church officials; the Cantoras, women who sing the chants in the choir; and several others that perform custodial activities throughout the performance.

Some performances during the Easter Festival have origins which doubtless precede Christian influences. The Pascola (i.e., "old man of the fiesta") dances to the alternate accompaniment of the drum and flute, and the harp and violin. He wears a cotton blanket sashed with a

Yaqui Chapayeka

belt of sleighbells around his hips. Barefooted, he wears cocoon rattles around his ankles. He carries a rattle that he sounds by beating it against his open palm. His long hair is tied with a red ribbon, and he wears a black wooden mask decorated with white designs. The performance of the Deer Dancer is also well known at this time. The Deer Dancer wears a dark-colored shawl around his hips over pants rolled up almost to the knees. He wears cocoon rattles on his ankles and a deer-hoof rattle belt. On his head over a white cloth is a deer head, worn during the dance performance. The Deer Dancer performs to the accompaniment of percussion music made by scraper rasps, which use gourds as resonators; and a half-gourd is beaten while held in a pan of water, which serves as a resonator.

Throughout Lent—and dramatically portrayed on such occasions as the Friday evening services when the community celebrates the Way of the Cross, which is established as a path around the village area immediately surrounding the church and plaza—the forces of evil slowly engender more and more power. By Holy Week, they have become so strong that they begin assaulting the church in an effort to take control of it. On Wednesday (Tenebrae), the Fariseos begin their search for Jesus. On Thursday, they chase Viejito, an old man who is like Jesus. They taunt and make fun of him but do not kill him, for he is old. They continue to search for Jesus and finally find him (a sculpted representation) in a cottonwood bower, which has been constructed to represent the Garden of Gethsemane. They destroy the bower and capture the figure of Jesus, taking him to the church, where he is held captive while the Chapayekas stand guard over him all night. In control of the church with Jesus as their captive, the forces of evil seem to have triumphed. There is apparent confirmation of this on Good Friday, when Jesus is crucified and entombed.

But the triumph of evil is short, for in the predawn hours of Saturday morning, the Fariseos discover that Jesus has risen. With the resurrection, the forces of good slowly begin to reassert themselves. A new fire ceremony is celebrated. Later a straw figure of Judas, the betrayer of Jesus dressed like a Chapayeka, is borne by the Chapayekas on the back of a burro around the Way of the Cross but in the wrong direction. Judas is fastened to a pyre near the church cross in the plaza. The Chapayekas dance before this figure who is their chief to honor him. Sensing their loss of power, the Fariseos repeatedly launch attacks upon the church, but they are repelled by flowers and confetti thrown at them. Flowers and confetti are the blood of Christ transformed, and they are deadly ammunition against evil. Repelled again and again, the Fariseos (including the masked Chapayekas) finally run back to the Judas pyre. Here they remove their masks and throw them, along with their swords and daggers, upon the pyre. Guided by their kin and with heads covered, they run back to the church to be rededicated to Jesus and to receive flowers. The Judas pyre is ignited, and all these symbols of evil are consumed in the flames. The Pascolas, Matachinis, and the Deer Dancer celebrate the victory by dancing in front of the church the rest of the day.

Yaqui deer dancer

155
*Tradition and
Change in
Native
American
Religions*

On Easter Sunday during a final procession with the infant Jesus, the Fariseos make final assaults on the church. Again they are repelled and finally discard their weapons (this time only switches and twigs) in surrender. The procession continues around the plaza, and the holy figures are placed on the altar. The people form a large circle near the church cross, and the head Maestro delivers a sermon from the center of the circle about the meaning of the Easter ceremony. Then the Fariseos and Caballeros go around the circle three times saying farewell until the following year.[4]

Quite in contrast to the response of the Rio Grande Pueblos to Christianity, we observe in the Yaqui Easter Festival what appears to be a complex integration of native ceremonial dance practices with Christian liturgy and beliefs. We might believe that the Christian elements and beliefs tend to dominate, but in the folk style in which the pageant is performed, there is obvious evidence of the festival's continuity with some aspects of the native tradition. Yet things are not always what they appear to be, and we are in for a few surprises and a greatly reshaped understanding of the Yaqui Easter Festival when we see it in terms of its history, which stems from Sonora, Mexico, more than three centuries ago. Let us briefly retrace this story.[5]

At the time of first contact with the Spanish in 1533, the Yaquis were the northernmost of the Cahita tribes who lived along rivers in Sonora, Mexico. Their well-developed military abilities at the time of this first contact enabled them to repel a party of slave raiders under the leadership of Diego de Guzmán. Yet while the Yaquis could act in concert when threatened militarily, they apparently had no general tribal organization. They lived in perhaps 80 rancherias, each consisting of about 300 or 400 persons, spread along the flood plain of the Yaqui River. Their principal mode of sustenance was cultivation, yet they maintained control of large areas of land from which they could supplement their livelihood by hunting and gathering wild foodstuffs.

Little is known of their religion at this early time, but it is believed that they sought individual visions in order to acquire personal spirits. Shamanic practices focused upon curing and hunting. These shamanic performances were individually conducted affairs, while ceremonials involving the community were concerned with war, hunting, and initiation.

During the 16th century, there was little contact between the Yaquis and the Spanish. By 1590, Jesuit missionaries had worked their way up the west coast of Mexico as far as the Cahita tribes. The Spanish were gradually moving in this direction in conquest of lands but did not reach the Yaquis until 1608, when they suffered defeat by the Yaquis.

They suffered another defeat in 1610, as the Yaquis made clear that they would not submit to Spanish power. For almost three centuries, the Yaqui people would retain something of their autonomy.

While the Yaquis did not want to be under Spanish rule, they did not reject all Spanish influence. Soon after defeating the Spanish military effort, the Yaquis asked that Jesuit missionaries be sent to them. The request was fulfilled in 1617, when two Jesuit missionaries arrived. The Yaquis received them enthusiastically and immediately engaged in extensive transformations of their culture as they accepted the innovations introduced by the Jesuits. Within two years, all 30,000 Yaquis had been baptized. Within six years, the eighty rancherias had been consolidated into eight pueblos or towns built around the mission churches, the plan modeled upon the Jesuits' idea of European towns. This town structure rapidly became deeply embedded in Yaqui tradition. By 1700, their mythology maintained the sacredness of the towns and the surrounding land. Each town was said to be founded by a prophet on the mandate of the gods.

The Jesuit missionaries maintained long-term commitments to the Yaqui people. They learned their language and taught the Yaqui people to read and write not only Spanish but their own language. They made little attempt to suppress the native traditions, focusing their concerns more on the translation of prayers, the mass, and Scripture into Yaqui language. Certain Yaqui men were given positions in the church and assisted in the celebration of mass. Some also aided Jesuit attempts to force the Yaquis to attend mass.

Another important facet of the Jesuit approach was their teaching of music and introduction of dramatic presentations of Christian belief. These were New World adaptations of the widespread European miracle plays, which dramatized such things as the Seven Sorrows of the Virgin Mary and the Passion of Jesus. Besides the Passion Play itself, the Yaquis performed others, such as one that told the story of the first Indian conversion in Mexico.

For more than a century, the Yaquis had a peculiar relationship with the Spanish. They were unique in successfully defending themselves against Spanish colonial efforts and remained free of influence by civil authorities. Yet they enthusiastically undertook extensive innovations under the guidance of a few Jesuit missionaries.

Not until the 1730s, when some Spaniards had established themselves as large agricultural proprietors in the land area adjacent to Yaqui territory, did the Yaqui people begin to feel the pressure of Spanish civil interests. These Spaniards were not sympathetic to the

157
*Tradition and
Change in
Native
American
Religions*

Jesuit mission program, and their anti-Jesuit disputes led to the Yaqui revolt in 1740. The great military strength of the Yaquis initially permitted them to scourge the area of Spaniards, but the Spanish strength was finally too great, and the Yaquis went down in defeat in a battle that may have claimed as many as 5,000 Yaqui lives. The Yaqui territory then became an outpost of New Spain. They continued for a time their relationships with the Jesuits and expanded their program of innovation, which included establishment of an organized school system that extended even to advanced schooling in Mexico City of select graduates of the Jesuit school.

Finally in 1767, just 150 years after their arrival, the Jesuit missionaries were expelled from the Yaqui towns. The Spanish-Yaqui differences had become too great. But in this period of a century and a half, the Yaquis had undergone transformations that had completely reshaped their culture and religious traditions. They had accepted a host of techniques and forms from the Jesuits; in many cases, they invested these with their own set of meanings quite different from those taught by the Jesuits. For example, the Jesuits made extensive use of the cross. The Yaquis quickly accepted it but associated it with a female deity, whom they called "Our Mother." They treated the cross as a female deity; at the spring festival that became known as Finding the Holy Cross, they dressed it and gave it appropriate ornamentation. This identification of the cross as a mother goddess still exists.

According to Edward Spicer, a longtime student of Yaqui history and culture, the Jesuit influence in transforming the Yaqui way of life during this period amounted to an extensive enrichment of the content of Yaqui culture. The precontact concerns and world view persisted but were enriched by acceptance of Spanish-introduced forms of expression. Areas that underwent perceivable change in Yaqui tradition during this period were three. There was a decrease in warfare activities; the Yaquis did not take up arms against anyone from 1620 until the Yaqui revolt in 1740. Second, since the Jesuit missions had to be supported by Yaqui labor, the considerable change in farming techniques resulted in increased production, which created a shift from subsistence farming to production of a surplus to support a modest export economy. The third area of change—intensified ceremonial activities—was associated with the greater concentration of peoples in the towns and with Jesuit influence. Concentration of population was accompanied by pressures to engage in certain governmental innovations.

The great loss of life that occurred when the Yaqui revolt was put down by the Spaniards in 1740 marked the beginning of a gradual decline in Yaqui population and autonomy during a period when the Spanish government asserted increasing pressure. The Yaquis, who never simply gave up the idea of their autonomy, shifted their focus again to military activities. Population loss resulted from a number of difficulties. They were visited by epidemics of smallpox and measles, which they had somehow escaped before. Their military efforts frequently resulted in considerable loss of life. People began to leave the Yaqui towns to work in mines and at other jobs, becoming assimilated into other populations in Sonora.

Even with the Jesuit missionaries gone, they retained and developed their ceremonial activities, which had been partly derived from Christian ritual forms. But they could not maintain the high level of agricultural production achieved during the mission period. While they attempted to produce crops adequate for self-sufficiency, often even this much could not be accomplished.

Threats to the existence of the Yaquis, especially to the autonomy of the religiously sanctioned towns, generated much effort to develop methods by which the communities could become highly integrated and protected against outside influences. Maintaining autonomy was increasingly difficult, however, and finally became impossible with the military defeat of the Yaquis in 1887. Their leader Cajeme was executed. This defeat resulted from, among many things, the decline in Yaqui population and the rise in strength of the Mexican government, which had been established in 1820. But development of the mechanisms for integrating and maintaining the culture continued even beyond the existence of the eight Yaqui towns. These mechanisms rested firmly upon a highly developed system of religious beliefs and practices. There is much evidence concerning this system as it existed in the 1880s, indicating that it was richly developed and vital to the very identity of the Yaquis.

After their defeat in 1887, the Yaquis entered a period of history that saw the people widely dispersed from their sacred homelands. Their lands were divided and distributed to Mexican settlers, and many Yaquis were deported and relocated by the Mexican government. Although guerilla activities continued for a long time after their defeat, the Yaqui communities no longer existed; the people had been dispersed in every direction. Many lost their identity as Yaquis, but others persisted. Some groups crossed the border into the United States, and by the turn of the century Yaqui settlements had been established at three locations in Arizona. Others were located in Sonora. Not until

1906 did the Yaquis in Arizona realize that they had been granted political asylum and could reinstitute the Easter Festival and other customs that were part of Yaqui tradition. The revival was partial but Yaqui nonetheless, and the tradition continues to live in the Easter Festival still celebrated every year in the Arizona Yaqui communities.

It is important at this point to review Yaqui religion in the 1880s, when it stood behind the reestablishment and continuity of Yaqui tradition in Arizona. By the 1880s, the Yaquis had enjoyed a period of a century and a half without the presence of missionaries. It was during this period that the religion of the eight towns took fullest shape. The eight towns were closely integrated, and the religion may be understood in terms of four cults that took responsibility for specialized ceremonial activities. These activities were sanctioned because of their origins in sacred history.

The Yaqui tradition holds that Jesus was born in the Yaqui town Belem and that he went about the Yaqui country curing and helping the people, who were constantly threatened by evil beings. The principal religious order of the Yaquis was the cult of Jesus, commonly called "the Lord," or "*El Señor*." This cult was comprised of two societies: the Horsemen, who were devotees of Christ the child; and the Judases, devotees of the crucified Christ. This cult was responsible for the major festival of the year, the Easter Festival. Of central importance here is that the stories of Jesus were given a geographical place in the sacred territory of the Yaquis. This served to establish the Yaqui identity and to help defend them and their lands against the encroachments of non-Yaquis.

An indigenous religious belief of northern Mexican peoples had focused on a female deity associated with the rainy season of growth. Upon the introduction of Christian symbolic forms, this belief engaged the figure of Mary, mother of Jesus, in the formation of what became, by the late 19th century, a cult of the Virgin. The figure upon which this cult focused was called both "Our Mother" and "Blessed Mary." She was represented both by the wooden or plaster Catholic images and by a rough cross of mesquite, which was dressed and ornamented in special devotion during the spring. This cult remained strongly associated with spring and was marked by the characteristic Yaqui use of bright colors and flowers. The most important devotees of the cult were the Matachin dancers, who vowed service to the Virgin in return for help in curing. Their dance was originally introduced by the Jesuits as part of the drama that depicted the first conversion of a Mexican Indian; but this dramatic context had been lost by the late 19th century and was replaced by devotion to the emergent figure of the Virgin.

The cult of the dead centered upon Yaqui interest by means of the ancestral dead, whom they remembered in books of family records handled in ritual ways at fiestas. Monthly gatherings at the village graveyards and special celebrations at the annual All Souls Feast in November integrated this cult with the other two.

The fourth cult was perhaps an aspect of the cult of the Virgin. Its patroness was the Virgin of Guadalupe, the patron saint of Mexico. This cult was primarily concerned with military activities.

The ideology and beliefs of these cults were based on or derived from the aboriginal tradition; but they were influenced, especially in form, by the Christian and European innovations introduced by the Jesuits more than two centuries earlier. In the period that ended in 1887, a constant presence at ceremonials throughout the year were the Pascola and Deer Dancers, who maintained direct continuity with the aboriginal Yaqui tradition. Their performances were unlike those of the other cults. They served in the capacity of clowns and entertainers, and maintained the lively art form of storytelling. It was doubtless the Pascola and Deer Dancers who maintained the aesthetic and cultural vitality in the Yaqui towns through their music, dance, and stories. Notably, the Yaquis had a complex oral tradition suffused with historical and mythic events by the 1880s. The many difficult events in their history were remembered in stories that collectively comprised a narrative of Yaqui suffering.

By 1887, when the Yaqui towns in Sonora fell, they enjoyed a new religious culture that had emerged from a period of development beginning at the time of the Jesuit missions more than a century and a half earlier. This religious culture arose in a historical process directed primarily by the Yaqui people themselves. They had invited and accepted broad changes, but they had generally controlled what had influenced them. The emergent religious tradition was a fusion of select elements from their aboriginal tradition and from the Christian-Spanish contacts they had sought out. The religious tradition as it appeared in the late 19th century could scarcely be called Christian. Even though Christian terminology and symbols were widely used, these seem to have been so extensively transformed by Yaqui tradition that they cannot correctly be considered as maintaining continuity with Christianity in the Americas.

With this history as background, we may now look anew at the Yaqui religious tradition as it appears in the celebration of Easter. Once reestablished as communities in Arizona, the Yaquis sought a revival of their old traditions. The cults, except for the cult of the Virgin of Guadalupe, were revived in somewhat truncated form. The major ceremonial that was revived was the Easter Festival, which was conducted by the cult of Jesus (the Fariseos). This was the revival of the primarily non-Christian tradition upon the sacred image of the culture as it had been developed in the eight towns—the sacred history and landscape of Yaqui culture.

Yaqui communities were generally well accepted and have even been supported by the communities of Tucson and Phoenix, to which they are neighbors. The Yaquis had to depend largely upon wage labor to support themselves and thus accepted a cash economy. They have found themselves in constant contact with non-Yaquis. In the context of these major cultural transformations, the Yaqui acceptance of Christian beliefs has almost totally occurred during the period since resettlement. Still, the Yaqui church is not recognized by the Catholic church.

During Easter Week, the distinction between Yaqui and Christian belief takes the startling form described at the beginning of this section. The Yaqui and Spanish Catholic churches stand side by side in Guadalupe. During Easter Week, the plaza before the Christian church is filled with the bright lights and happy noises of a carnival; while in the plaza in front of the Yaqui church, the crucifixion and resurrection of Jesus are dramatically enacted through dance and music; and the comrades of Judas—the representatives of evil—are once again overcome by the brightly colored flowers—the blood of Jesus—that are victoriously hurled at them by the people.

THE PLAINS TRIBES

The horse-mounted, war-bonneted figure of the Plains tribesman has been a dominant image of the "Indian" in America. This romantic image has only recently begun to fade from the screens of our motion-picture theaters. As a noble profile, this figure once appeared on the nickel with a buffalo on its flip side. It is this image that stands predominant in the minds of most Americans as representative of that aboriginal race of noble savages who lived in tipis upon the high plains, following the endless herds of buffalo in their timeless, nomadic ways. This is the image tied to the whooping and scalping savagery directed toward innocent settlers and falling before the gunfire of the U.S. Cavalry.

While the image has some real basis in Plains cultures and American history, the archaic, timeless attributes with which we identify it are far from accurate. A broad general review of the history of the Plains tribes will serve not only to correct these impressions but will introduce us to a complex past, in which the religions of these tribes were constantly engaged in change and innovation to meet rapidly shifting needs. We will see that this noble image, as well as the religions we most closely identify with Plains traditions, are partly products of the European presence in America.

To begin the story, we can project a general picture of the culture types that lived on the prairies and plains 1,000 years ago.[6] Evidence concerning these cultures reveals the influence of several culture types and the necessity of adapting to ecological conditions. Along the Missouri River and its tributaries were sedentary corn-growing peoples. They spent most of their time near their villages tending their crops, but they also engaged in hunting on a seasonal basis. They had been influenced in both agriculture and religion by the high Mexican cultures, doubtless introduced to them by cultures bordering east of the plains region along the Mississippi River. These influences had spread northward from Mexico along the Mississippi. Among these peoples living along the Missouri River were the ancestors of the Mandan, believed to have been the first users of the famous feathered war bonnets. Here too were the ancestors of the Pawnee, who probably originated the calumet or "peacepipe." Ecological conditions were a large factor in keeping these tribes confined to the river corridors, along which they could grow corn and occasionally hunt to provide for their livelihood.

To the far western side of the Plains near the Rocky Mountains lived groups of nomadic buffalo hunters. Because of the ecological conditions, few of these groups existed at this early time, and they were widely scattered throughout the area. Their religious patterns were not elaborate and probably focused upon individual needs in ways like vision fasting, thus emulating mythic culture heroes.

During the centuries that followed, increasing intermingling and interchange occurred among these cultures; but the most significant appearance in the Northern Plains did not occur until the 17th century—the appearance of the peoples we commonly know by the name Sioux. Before this time, these peoples had lived for a long time on the prairies and in the woodlands of today's Minnesota and Wisconsin. Those who lived in the western part of this area were hunters; those in the east were hunters, fishers, and corn farmers. These are the peoples that we most closely associate with the war-bonneted image. Around the beginning of the 17th century, the Ojibwa, who lived adjacent to the Sioux, armed themselves with guns they received from white fur traders—and, around 1640, they succeeded in evicting the Sioux from their area, thus forcing them to take residence in the area of the northern plains. Displaced from their homelands and way of life, these peoples became nomadic and lived by plundering the villages along the Missouri. In the early 18th century, horses, which had been introduced by the Spanish in the Southwest and Southern Plains, began to arrive in the Northern Plains in sufficient numbers to permit a major transformation of the Sioux tribes. By integrating the horse into their nomadic way of life, they achieved a power that soon brought them into commanding control of the Northern Plains region. The village cultures entered a period of decline.

The Sioux peoples demonstrated their great capacity for innovation and creative borrowing not only in terms of subsistence patterns and life ways but also in religion. The old fertility rites, which were the center of the corn-growing cultures, were transformed to fit the needs of the nomadic hunting peoples. Their central concern with corn was complemented by, and shifted to, a concern for buffalo and other game, while the communal orientation was complemented with a concern for the individual by giving emphasis to vision experiences. The result of these religious innovations was what we know as the Sun Dance, which is the most common and typical of religious practice of the Plains tribes. The Sun Dance, performed annually, was a ceremonial effecting a world renewal that promoted prosperity for the tribe.

By the middle of the 19th century, the nomadic tribes of the Northern Plains, especially the Sioux, had developed a way of life that dominated the Plains area. Their life way was linked with the horse and the buffalo, both of which had become dominant religious symbols. Their religious practices were focused upon individual vision experiences, shamanic practices associated with hunting and curing, and the great Sun Dance ceremonial, which had established itself as a tradition rooted in the primordial past. Yet, from the perspective of American history, we can see that the presence of the Sioux in the Plains area and the way in which their religion had developed resulted, though indirectly, from the presence of Europeans in America; the horse, by which they had come to such great power, was itself a European introduction. This fact, of course, takes nothing away from the significance of the religions and cultures of the Plains peoples; indeed, it celebrates their enormous capacities to engage in a history of development and radical innovation that permitted them not only to survive, but to achieve heights of cultural and religious development.

The first half of the 19th century was simultaneously a period of great strength for the northern Plains cultures and of the increasing presence of American settlers. This threatening pressure was being felt by Native Americans throughout the United States. The Removal Act of 1830 resulted in displacement of the populations commonly known as the Five Civilized Tribes (because of their great efforts to acculturate themselves to European-American ways) from the southeastern United States to the Oklahoma territory. Sporadic military efforts by Plains tribes attempted to repel the American settlers, but such efforts eventually proved futile. As other means of resistance also began to fail, millenarian movements based upon messages revealed to prophets began to erupt and spread among the tribes. In the 18th century, a prophet arose among the Delaware and foretold that the land taken from them by the French and English would be returned to them by divine intervention. He told his people that, in the meantime, they should behave themselves, give up drinking alcohol, and act like brothers to one another.[7]

In the early years of the 19th century, the Shawnee prophet Tenskwataya, brother of Tecumseh, arose and made similar predictions, advocating a reform ethic. He traveled widely and attempted to build an intertribal confederacy, but he was killed in the War of 1812, and his efforts never developed.[8]

Numerous other prophetic movements arose, and religious organizations such as the Indian Shakers of the Puget Sound area took shape as a result. In the 1850s and 1860s, another movement arose around Smohalla, a Wanapum in today's state of Washington, whose alleged statements about the "Indians'" relationship to the earth as mother have been so often quoted. This movement, facing the devastation and cultural deprivation being suffered, focused upon the belief in an impending destruction and renewal of the world, during which the dead would return. The performance of a dance based on imitation of the dances of the dead conjoined with millennial expectations gave rise to the Ghost Dance movement of 1870, which was widely practiced throughout the northwest area.[9] These prophetic and millenarian movements were akin to the Ghost Dance of 1890, the best known of such movements, which was widely practiced among the Plains tribes; there is doubtless an historical connection between this movement and the earlier Ghost Dance movement.[10]

The origin of this movement was not in the Plains but in Nevada. A

165
*Tradition and
Change in
Native
American
Religions*

Paiute by the name of Wovoka, who lived on the Walker Lake Reservation, was its source. Wovoka had participated in the Ghost Dance of 1870, and he may have been familiar with Shaker religion. His background was somewhat characteristic of Native American prophets. He learned something of Paiute shamanism from his father, and he practiced it among his people. He also had considerable contact with Americans. He worked for a settler family who named him Jack Wilson, acquiring from this family some knowledge of Christian theology and Scripture. Although he traveled little outside of the area of his home, he served as a bridge between cultures, typifying prophetic figures in this regard.

In the winter of 1888–89, Wovoka became ill. Coincident with a solar eclipse that alarmed the Paiute people in January, he reported having had a vision in which he had gone to the spirit world and visited with the dead. He had received a millennial message and had been instructed on what the people should do in preparation for the coming end of the world. They should perform trance dances and uphold right living by not drinking, fighting, or quarrelling. Wovoka's message spread rapidly, especially among the Plains tribes, who even sent delegations to visit Wovoka in order to receive his message first hand. The Ghost Dance of 1890 brought to many cultures a message of hope in a world of increasing despair. It reflected the effects of the major transformations forced upon the Plains peoples in the decade ending in 1890.[11]

In June of 1876 came the Battle of the Little Bighorn, in which Custer suffered his defeat. The Sioux still asserted the vitality of their culture. In the summer, autumn, and winter of 1876, the Plains tribes continued to defend themselves and their way of life against American troops but with decreasing success. Many Sioux surrendered in May of 1877. Bands of hostiles managed to remain free until 1881, when they too finally surrendered. The Sioux were promptly placed on reservations.

On reservations, the traditional means of attaining prestige, wealth, and rank vanished. There was no war, no hunting, and no raiding. The traditional tribal economy collapsed, and this collapse forced radical changes in diet, clothing styles, and housing. The people had no choice but to accept rations and annuities from the U.S. government, which supported them in this way while attempting to turn the people into farmers like the settlers. Because of the climate, land conditions, and temperament of the people, this effort failed miserably. The native peoples were forced to undergo political reorganization in order to have a means of meeting white demands, and this conflicted with the traditional political organization, which itself could no longer function.

In 1883, a policy set forth by the Bureau of Indian Affairs prohibited the practice of the Sun Dance, as well as other feasts and dances. Christian missionaries, especially the Episcopalians, entered to fill the gap by quickly establishing churches and schools throughout the reservations, thus introducing Christian beliefs and practices and white education. The decade of the 1880s saw completion of the railroad across the plains, serving to bring increasing numbers of settlers and visitors to the region.

The famous Buffalo Bill's Wild West Show, which also began in 1883, exploited Native Americans as curiosities for audiences throughout the United States, Canada, and Europe. Even Sitting Bull traveled with the show in 1885. The show was a major influence in spreading the Plains costume and war-bonneted images that are still familiar to us. It served even to teach Native Americans how they were supposed to dress and act in conformance with their growing awareness of being "Indians." In the show, members of many cultures that had been enemies came together and found a common bond in their "Indianness."

Another notable event of the decade was the establishment of Indian schools such as Carlisle of Pennsylvania in 1887. Young people from many tribes were sent to these schools to be educated. The common bonds they acquired, accompanied by education in the ways of the dominant culture, prepared many of these students to lead movements for the preservation and protection of the rights of all Native Americans. The efforts of these early pan-Indian movements have actively continued to the present.

The decade of the 1880s saw the entire collapse of the traditional Sioux religion and way of life. Forced innovations had been introduced on a massive scale. The Ghost Dance came at a time of desperate need, broadly felt among the Plains peoples. It was quickly accepted and practiced by many as the last hope for recovery of the old ways. Throughout 1890, the peoples participated in the Ghost Dance in anticipation of the end of the world, a return of the dead, and a rebirth into the world as it had been of old. But this spark of hope contained, at least for the Sioux, a militant element; for it was prophesied that those who wore special "ghost shirts" would be impervious to the penetration of bullets. This made the U.S. government troops nervous, and in this context came the senseless killing of hundreds of Sioux men, women, and children on December 29, 1890, at Wounded Knee Creek. The spark of hope carried by the Ghost Dance was snuffed out with the lives of these people.

167
*Tradition and
Change in
Native
American
Religions*

The 1890 Ghost Dance movement, which had sought restoration of the physical, social, and cultural conditions of the past, had failed to obtain these goals; but it played a major role in bringing together and unifying tribes that had previously had little association. It diffused among these tribes new religious patterns, which were adapted in a variety of ways to maintain some continuity with the old religious traditions. In the decade of the 1880s, more extensive travel by Native Americans and concentrated contact with white culture (especially in terms of religion and education), coupled with the loss of tribal functions in warfare and hunting, promoted the rise of an "Indian" as distinct from a "tribal" identity among the Plains peoples.[12]

As the Plains tribes entered the 20th century, they were forced to adjust to a very complex situation. Prevented from following their old way of life, they found it impossible simply to import a new tradition. Three main paths were entered by various groups, and these paths were often combined. One path was to hold to those practices that have threads of continuity with the old tradition and try to revive them as much as possible. Along this path, the Sun Dance and other ceremonial activities were eventually revived. Another path was to encourage pan-Indian identity as much as possible and to develop traditions that were "Indian" in character. Numerous political organizations and ceremonial practices like the powwow arose as a result. Another path was the attempt to drop tribal and "Indian" identity as much as possible and to assimilate completely into white culture. One step in this direction is the acceptance of Christianity and the acquisition of employment apart from the native reservations and communities.

One means of accommodating some aspects of all three paths was found in peyote religion, which became very widespread in the Plains early in this century and which has continued to spread among Native Americans to the present. As the most significant pan-Indian religion of this century, we must consider it further.[13]

The cactus commonly known as peyote (*Lophophora williamsii*) has been long used for religious purposes by Native Americans in Mexico, where the cactus grows. Its use was introduced to the Kiowa and Comanche tribes in the southern plains about 1870. By the time of the Ghost Dance movement of 1890, it was still not widespread, but the pan-Indian awareness and broadening of friendly relationships among Native Americans throughout the Plains area established conditions conducive to its great diffusion. Certainly peyote religion did not spread among tribes in North America at anything near the feverish rate that the Ghost Dance religion had. During the first two decades of

Fancy dancer at a pow wow

this century, peyote religion slowly grew among tribes throughout the Plains and surrounding areas.

An important diffusionist mechanism for peyote religion was the traveling peyote leader. A number of such figures traveled from tribe to tribe to spread their version of the religion and its ritual performances. One such leader was Quannah Parker, a Comanche chief and famous war leader. His mother, who was white, had been captured as a child and raised as a Comanche. He held out against white pressures until 1875. Upon his surrender, he set about establishing a new way of life for his people, a way that would combine Comanche and Anglo-American ways. He prospered as a farmer and rancher. Encouraging the pursuit of education, he sent three of his children to Carlisle. He became a friend of President Theodore Roosevelt, who visited Parker and went on hunting trips with him. In 1884, Parker became seriously ill. When he recovered, he attributed his cure to peyote. This made him a convert to peyote religion, and he entered upon a lifelong effort to spread the practice of peyote religion among native peoples. Because Parker did not abandon his efforts to accommodate Anglo-American culture in peyote religion, peyote beliefs and practices thus incorporated some Christian elements.

Another figure instrumental in the spread of peyotism was John Wilson, who was Delaware and Caddo with one-quarter French. Wilson established widespread contact among Native American cultures in the last half of the 19th century. He had taken up peyote religion in 1880 when, subject to a number of revelations under the influence of peyote, he was given a body of moral and religious teachings that included instructions for the ceremonial procedures and preparation of the paraphernalia. Central to such preparation was the construction of a moon-shaped altar, with which his version of peyote came to be identified. Wilson was engaged in peyote religion at the time of the Ghost Dance, which he accepted as well, becoming a leader of the Ghost Dance among the Caddo. After the Ghost Dance movement had run its course, Wilson returned to his efforts to spread the peyote way until his death in 1901. Wilson's version of peyote religion also incorporated many Christian elements.

As peyote religion came to be widely established by the end of the first decade of this century, it began to draw fire from U.S. authorities. A string of legal efforts, which have yet to cease, has attempted to prevent Native Americans from practicing peyote religion. The attack has centered on the use of the peyote cactus.

Native Americans who had to fight these legal battles began to incorporate themselves as churches in order to gain a firm legal status and to find shelter under the protection of religious liberty guaranteed by the U.S. Constitution. The first incorporation under the name "Native American Church" occurred in Oklahoma in 1918. Federal legislation introduced to prohibit the use of peyote failed to be enacted

Peyote meeting, Native American Church

into law, but several states outlawed its use that year. More and more groups of peyotists incorporated in order to obtain a churchlike base upon which to maintain the legality of their religious practices.

We can now see that peyote religion could enter any of the three paths of accommodation, even combining them in varying degrees. Most distinctive is the "Indian" character of peyote religion. It is not a religious practice introduced by European-American culture, and it has a history deeply rooted in aboriginal America. Yet it is "Indian" as opposed to "tribal" in character. This development has accommodated the growing pan-Indian awareness throughout this period in history. The most widespread feature that distinguishes peyote religion, aside from the use of peyote, is the ethic it has preached and strongly supported. This ethic focuses on problems that Native Americans recognize as threatening their very existence. First among these is prohibition of the use of alcohol.

While in many cases the old, traditional religions could no longer be practiced, the practice of peyote religion was not difficult. It required only the acquisition of peyote and a few simple items of ritual paraphernalia. Furthermore, peyote religion could be construed as continuous with the old ways. The acquisition of visions under the influence of peyote was linked with the older practice of seeking visions on such occasions as puberty, preparation for war, and initiation into societies. The use of peyote has also been widely associated with medicine and thus carries on the native healing practices.

Finally the practice of peyote religion could either exclude Christian beliefs and practices or extensively incorporate them. The use of peyote has commonly been defended as corresponding to the Eucharist in Christianity. Jesus has been commonly identified with the spirit of peyote. Quannah Parker, for example, is reported to have said, "The white man goes into his church house and talks *about* Jesus, but the Indian goes into his tipi and talks *to* Jesus."[14]

Peyote religion is most remarkable in its capacity for meeting the complex needs of Native Americans throughout North America during this most difficult period in their history. It carries on the traditions of ritual curing and the seeking of individual visions; it has created a new ethic focused on the rejection of alcohol; it has created a new base for communal organization to support the continuity of tribal identity; it fosters the growth of "Indian" identity; and it even provides for the embracing and nativizing of elements of Christianity. While all of these factors were fit into a matrix for rejection of the non-"Indian" world, peyote religion nonetheless has been capable of establishing an appearance that has permitted it to survive, although under constant threats.[15]

The threats and criticisms of peyote religion have come not only from European-American culture but also from staunchly traditional elements within tribal cultures that have seen it as too accommodating to nonnative ways.[16]

CONCLUSION

The three examples we have considered in this chapter are too few to enable us to draw any general conclusions about the nature of the history and historical processes of Native American religions. They do, however, serve to focus our general attention on several areas of general concern.

Language plays a central role in the maintenance of tradition. By means of language, we have been able to distinguish various Native American tribes and to trace some lines of the prehistoric period. We saw some aspects of this importance of language in our three examples. The approach of the Franciscans and Jesuits was distinguished in one way by their interest or noninterest in native languages. The Franciscans generally did not learn the Pueblo languages, and their greater hostility to native religious practices is compatible with that disinterest. In such a context, it would have been difficult for the Pueblo tribes to have given more than compartmentalized responses to the missionaries. The Jesuits were deeply interested in learning and translating Christian materials into the Yaqui language, thus providing a context for greater assimilation of European symbols—and later, ideas—by the Yaqui. We also noticed the importance that European languages, particularly Spanish and English, have played in providing a lingua franca for Native American tribes, thus giving to peoples who otherwise did not communicate in frequent or friendly ways a commonality in language. This development accompanied and helped create their sense of a shared oppression and identity as "Indian." A common language has been fundamental to the development of pan-Indianism.

In these examples, there appears to be a relationship between the extent and character of intercultural contact and the reaction made by the traditions of these cultures. When cultures are threatened by oppressive forces, they apparently respond with a series of actions that serve to strengthen tradition and to intensify unity and identity. The degree and intensity of the oppressive forces is met by differing kinds of cultural responses; but at every level, religion plays a central role, for it is through religion that the world view and broad, meaning-giving perspectives are taught, effected, and developed. While the Rio Grande Pueblo peoples tended to retrench through their religious organizations and actions, they developed protective and isolationist mechanisms. The Yaqui extensively incorporated innovations from Spanish culture and religion, but they radically transformed these borrowings to maintain continuity with their own tradition. In the northern plains, we can observe a range of cultural influences, only indirectly European, that underpin the formulation of the Sun Dance tradition and later the Ghost Dance and peyote religions. We saw that when oppressive external pressures were reduced, acculturative processes were often accelerated.

Another important factor is the openness of a tradition to change. The Pueblo cultures appeared less open to the incorporation of change in tradition than our other examples. Perhaps this is related to the way of life. The Pueblos and the sedentary Plains tribes seem to have been less open to change and incorporation of elements borrowed from other cultures. They tended to seek isolation and protection. At the time of European contact, the Yaquis were a sedentary agriculturalist culture, but elements of a former hunting-type culture are evident in their concerns for individual visions, curing, and war. They, along with the Sioux, were the grander innovators in our examples.

We saw that economic factors are very significant. The difference between a subsistence and a money economy goes far beyond the simple economic aspects of alternative systems, for these systems reflect and influence the entire range of life. A subsistence economy encourages and even requires a closely unified community that may, with relative ease, avoid extensive contact with other cultures. Status, prestige, and human value are not linked to economic factors nearly as much as to knowledge, clan and society membership, and religious roles. On the other hand, a money economy encourages and even necessitates a much broader interaction among peoples, tending to discourage the intensive unity of small groups or tribes. Even more important, a money economy introduces a system of value, prestige, and meaning based on the possession of money and goods. The effects of such a system on religion and tradition are far-reaching.

We found in our examples that religious forms of expression—symbols, rituals, and stories—have histories. While these forms are commonly cast in the language of primordiality, the "in the beginning" time, they nonetheless are not survivals in the sense of being witnesses to some ancient past. We have observed how rapidly a tradition may reformulate its fundamental principles and perspectives and give them formal expression, the whole process being made possible by these religious forms. Hence the religious symbols of the great Sun Dance, the Yaqui Easter, and the Pueblo fiesta express the most basic and fundamental dimensions of reality—those dimensions formulated in the beginning by sanction and action of the deities. From another view, however, these symbols, rituals, and stories arise in the history of a tradition and are constantly subject to revision and alteration. And we must identify this process of change as a living tradition.

New forms of religion emerge to meet the exigencies of history. They help in the translation of world view and way of life. They help cultures to deal with the changes, gradual or radical, that are constantly encountered. These emerging religious forms, whether protective or accommodating, are essential to bridge that seeming paradox between constancy and change—a paradox that we describe by the word "tradition."

1. Adapted from Pliney E. Goddard, *Navaho Texts*, Anthropology Papers, vol. 34 (New York: American Museum of Natural History, 1933), p. 164.

2. The principal fiesta that honors St. Joseph is annually performed on September 19. For a description and general discussion of this fiesta, see Evon Z. Vogt, "A Study of the Southwestern Fiesta System as Exemplified by the Laguna Fiesta," *American Anthropologist* 57 (1955): 820–39.

3. The historic treatment here will be based upon the account by E. P. Dozier, "Rio Grande Pueblos," in *Perspectives in American Indian Culture Change*, ed. Edward H. Spicer (Chicago: University of Chicago Press, 1961), pp. 94–186.

4. Descriptions of recent Yaqui Easter Festivals may be found in Emily Brown, *The Passion of Pascua* (Tucson: Tucson Chamber of Commerce, 1941); and Muriel T. Painter, *The Yaqui Easter Ceremony* (Tucson: Tucson Chamber of Commerce, 1950).

5. The historic treatment here will be based on the account of Edward H. Spicer, "Yaqui," in *Perspectives in American Indian Culture Change*, ed. Edward H. Spicer (Chicago: University of Chicago Press, 1961), pp. 7–93. See also Edward H. Spicer, *Pascua, A Yaqui Village in Arizona* (Chicago: University of Chicago Press, 1940); and Edward H. Spicer, *Potam, A Yaqui Village in Sonora*, American Anthropological Association Memoir no. 77 (Menasha, Wisconsin, 1954).

6. For a review of this history, see Åke Hultkrantz, *Prairie and Plains Indians* (Leiden: E. J. Brill, 1973), pp. 1–4.

7. For a review of the larger history in which this prophet arose, see A. F. C. Wallace, "New Religious Beliefs Among the Delaware Indians 1600–1900," *Southwestern Journal of Anthropology* 12 (1956): 1–21.

8. See Benjamin Drake, *Life of Tecumseh and of his Brother the Prophet, with a historical Sketch of the Shawanoe Indians* (Philadelphia: Quaker City Publishing House, 1856).

9. See Cora DuBois, "The 1870 Ghost Dance," *Anthropological Records* 3 (1939): 1–151.

10. See especially James Mooney, *The Ghost Dance Religion and the Sioux Outbreak of 1890*, Smithsonian Institution, Bureau of American Ethnology, 14th Annual Report, part 2 (Washington, D.C., 1896).

11. For further discussion of the Sioux during the decade ending in 1890, see Robert M. Utley, *The Last Days of the Sioux Nation* (New Haven: Yale University Press, 1963), pp. 6–39.

12. For a study of modern pan-Indian movements, see Hazel W. Hertzberg, *The Search for an American Indian Identity* (Syracuse, N.Y.: Syracuse University Press, 1971).

13. For a comprehensive study of peyote movements, see Weston LaBarre, *The Peyote Cult* (New Haven: Yale University Publications in Anthropology, 1938; enlarged ed. New York: Schocken, 1969).

14. As quoted in Hazel W. Hertzberg, *The Search for an American Indian Identity*, p. 243.

15. For further analysis of these points, see Bryan R. Wilson, *Magic and the Millennium: A Sociological Study of Religious Movements of Protest among Tribal and Third-World Peoples* (New York: Harper & Row, 1973), pp. 414–41, 443–49.

16. For descriptions of peyote rituals, see LaBarre, *The Peyote Cult* (New York: Schocken, 1969), pp. 29–56.

CHAPTER 7

Concluding Remarks

In the Prologue of this book, I rejected use of the term "Indian" as an appropriate appellation for the peoples native to North America at the time of European contact. I rejected that term on the grounds of the inappropriate and incorrect images associated with it that have so extensively shaped not only the history of the European-American–Native American encounter but especially the understanding of Native American religions. I argued that the term arose through a situation in which a "we/they" distinction was needed. The term "Indian" in that context reflected a European construction that was little influenced by the actual attributes of aboriginal Americans. Consequently the term reflects more about Europeans than Native Americans.

It is now necessary, however, to qualify our use of the term "Indian" and to reverse somewhat the position I took in the Prologue. Beginning in the late 19th century and continuing to the present, as became clear in the previous chapter, peoples of various tribes in North America have increasingly found a level of identity commonly designated by the term "Indian." It is important for us to see that even in this new usage, the term arises to meet the same needs it served in the late 15th century, yet with the principals reversed. In this recent usage, the Native Americans have been the ones who have needed a "we/they" designation to distinguish them from Americans of European ancestry. Thus the term "Indian" was appropriated in the same manner and for the same reasons as was the English language—as a lingua franca upon which this identity is made possible.

I would caution that this is an identity that, for many Native Americans, continues to be secondary to their tribal identity; that is, many Native Americans continue to identify themselves first in terms of their own tribe and only secondarily—and often only in non-Indian or pan-Indian contexts—as "Indian." I would further caution that even in this pan-Indian usage, the term "Indian" is also affixed to an image that may not easily be borne out in the actual practices of the broad range of peoples to whom it refers. This image reverses the European image of the "Indian" by depicting Native Americans in the most positive light, often in contrast to the posited evils of European-American cultures cast in the image of the "white man."

It is important to note here that, in some cases, it is entirely appropriate to use the terms "Indian" and "Indian religion." These terms may correctly be used to refer to the recent shift from tribal to intertribal identity and to the development of religious forms that accompany this shift. It is also important to recognize that many Native American individuals today much prefer the use of the term "Indian," for it now has a history, in which is bound their identity and sense of value and meaning, that stems from well before their lifetimes. While in no way wishing to discount this preference, for the purposes of this introduction to Native American religions I have felt it essential to avoid aligning ourselves with any ethnic images and to consider them only insofar as they become a factor in the history of Native American religions.

The task of this book has been to chart the territory of Native American religions. Maps are necessarily pale and flat compared with the actual territory. But to provide some sense of the elevations and richness contained, I have presented a number of maps that reflect different levels and aspects of the terrain.

In Chapters 1 to 3, we considered some generally fundamental resources and tools with and upon which Native American religions are formulated and expressed. Chapter 1 concerned the character of the place, the symbolic language engaged in the formulation and expression of religious beliefs and world views. We considered the techniques and tools by which Native Americans map the internal aspects at the core of their religious views of the world. We found that these internal beliefs and views were given expression in a culture by symbolic forms, which we can come to appreciate by considering their arrangements of time and space.

Based on the belief that modes of communication constitute and underlie modes of thought and cultural patterns, we turned in Chapter

2 to the charting of nonliteracy as it shapes and characterizes certain aspects of Native American religious beliefs and expressions. Then we turned to consider Native American religious symbols beyond their role in the formulation and expression of knowledge and world view. We considered the effectiveness of symbols in Native American religious practices. Our concern in Chapter 3 was not only to understand how to approach religious symbols in order to understand them but to recognize that these symbols actually *do* something—that they have effects upon the lives and histories of Native Americans.

These three chapters equipped us with charts of some fundamental elements and materials through which Native American religions are expressed and perform their works. We then set out in Chapters 4 to 6 to chart several kinds of processes or patterns through which we could appreciate the organization and order of Native American religions. The first pattern, charted in Chapter 4, was the one corresponding with the individual life cycle—the life way. We considered major religious moments that correspond with the points of transition along this cycle. Rotating our perspective slightly in Chapter 5, we sought to construct maps of the religious elements that give cultures coherence and support their continuity as identifiable ways of life. Our final perspective in Chapter 6 brought us to the vantage of history. In these charts, we plotted the growth and development of religious traditions over time and considered the factors of constancy and change that constitute tradition.

In their outlines, these maps are indeed pale; but to enrich and give color to each, we have taken numerous excursions off the main lines onto the backroads and footpaths to observe cameo presentations of stories, rites, historical moments, ceremonies, individual views, images, and artifacts.

I have been unable to do justice to any particular religion—a task that could probably not be accomplished for any single tribe in an entire volume—nor have I attempted a very balanced treatment of the many tribes in North America. While I have aimed to include discussion of at least the major types of practice, forms of expression, and patterns of world view and ideology, none have been treated thoroughly, and doubtless some important ones have been omitted entirely. But these criteria have not been central to my task, which has been to offer a set of perspectives by which we may gain an introduction to Native American religions; and to present these perspectives so that they demonstrate an awareness of—if not entirely a freedom from—the evils of unexamined, inherited images of the subject. These, as all charts, are

preliminary to actual journeys into Native American territories as
preserved in libraries and museums—and as, even better, the territories continue to exist in the many communities of Native Americans.

179
*Concluding
Remarks*

SUGGESTIONS FOR FURTHER READING

The difficulty in advancing one's knowledge of Native American religions by reading is not in finding something of value to read but rather
in finding one's way into the almost overwhelming wealth of published material. One who seeks a general understanding of Native
American religions finds few general works, guides, and overviews to
aid in approaching the thousands of documents that report, often in
minutest detail, thousands of particulars for hundreds of tribes but
usually without offering much help in evaluating or interpreting these
items. Just one example makes the point. The Bureau of American
Ethnology began publishing field reports on an annual basis in 1888
and has also published a series of bulletins. These publications alone
fill one large bank of shelves; yet to find one's way into these
materials—and, more importantly finally, to emerge from them with
an understanding of Native American religions—is not a task for
which ready guides exist. This book has intended to provide some aid
in this endeavor, and would be incomplete without assisting the utili-
zation of this wealth of published materials.

Professor Åke Hultkrantz has contributed excellent and invaluable
bibliographical essays in "North American Indian Religion in the History of Research: A General Survey" (in four parts), *History of Religions*
6 (1966): 91–107 and 183–207; 7 (1967): 13–34 and 112–48. This is
updated in "The Contribution of the Study of North American Indian
Religions to the History of Religions" in Walter H. Capps, ed., *Seeing
with a Native Eye* (New York: Harper & Row, 1976), pp. 86–106. I have
made some bibliographical notations along with comments about the
research and teaching of Native American religions in Sam D. Gill,
"Native American Religions," *Council on the Study of Religion Bulletin* 9
(1978): 125–28; and in "Native American Religions: A Review Essay,"
Religious Studies Review 5/4 (1979): 251–58.

An important source of reference is Frederick W. Hodge, ed., *Handbook of American Indians North of Mexico* (New York: Pageant, 1960); a
new multivolume edition of this handbook is currently pending publication by the Smithsonian Institute. Some volumes have now begun to
appear. The Human Relations Area Files, which include many cultures

in North America, are also important sources, especially for comparative analyses. Accompanying these is George P. Murdock's *Ethnographic Bibliography of North America* (New Haven: Human Relations Area Files, 1975).

Valuable as a resource book is the recent work of Åke Hultkrantz, *The Religions of the American Indians* (Berkeley: University of California Press, 1979), which is organized in a typological and phenomenological manner for tribes of North America. For a selection of essays that interpret aspects of Native American religions, see Walter H. Capps, ed., *Seeing with a Native Eye* (New York: Harper & Row, 1976). A number of native texts are presented and discussed in Peggy V. Beck and A. L. Walters, *The Sacred: Ways of Knowledge, Sources of Life* (Tsaile, Ariz.: Navajo Community College Press, 1977).

Through these several sources, one should be able to gain access to the majority of primary materials including guides to the subject, perspective of the author, and value for religious studies of the published item.

Following are a few readings of particular interest that correlate with the major sections in this book.

Prologue

My concern in this section is not the history of the interrelationship between Native Americans and European-Americans but the European perspective that has shaped the way we have seen and understood Native American religions. I would suggest Edmundo O'Gorman's *The Invention of America* (Bloomington: Indiana University Press, 1961) as of central importance. Also enlightening are the works of Lewis Hanke, *Aristotle and the American Indians* (Bloomington: Indiana University Press, 1970); and *All Mankind Is One* (DeKalb: Northern Illinois University Press, 1974). Some aspects of this concern are also discussed by Robert F. Berkhofer, Jr., in *The White Man's Indian* (New York: Knopf, 1978).

Chapters 1 to 3

These three chapters have attempted to establish some perspectives and describe some interpretive tools for understanding and appreciating Native American religions. I know of no published materials that have applied these perspectives and tools to Native American religions. The Notes at the end of each chapter cite important works that have served as a base upon which I developed these perspectives. While the areas of application were not the essential concern of these chapters, nonetheless several areas were considered and I can suggest readings for these areas.

Relative to the subject of art and architecture, catalogs and collections are abundant. See, for example, Ralph T. Coe, *Sacred Circles: Two Thousand Years of North American Indian Art* (Kansas City, Mo.: Nelson Art Gallery, 1977); and Frederick J. Dockstader, *Indian Art in America* (Greenwich, Conn.: New York Graphic Society, 1961), and *Indian Art of the Americas* (New York: Museum of the American Indian, Heye Foundation, 1973).

The best guide to the oral traditions and folklore of North American cultures is Stith Thompson, *Tales of the North American Indians* (Bloomington: Indiana University Press, 1929). For bibliographies and studies of types of creation stories, see Anna Birgitta Rooth, "The Creation Myths of the North American Indians," *Anthropos* 52 (1957): 497–508; and Ermine Wheeler-Voegelin and Remedios W. Moore, "The Emergence Myth in Native North America," in *Studies in Folklore*, ed. W. E. Richmond (Bloomington: Indiana University Press, 1957).

Consult the chapter Notes for suggested readings on specific topics of examples mentioned in the chapter as well as for bibliography concerning the perspectives and tools presented.

Chapters 4 and 5

For information about the life cycle and sustenance patterns of Native American peoples, every ethnography of a Native American tribe is a source document. The cited *Handbooks* (especially the new Smithsonian Institute edition) and the Human Relations Area Files are invaluable for studies in this area. Beyond these, one may find a collection of data on several of these topics in George A. Pettitt, "Primitive Education in North America," *University of California Publications in American Archaeology and Ethnology* 43 (1946): 1–182; and in Harold E. Driver, *Girls' Puberty Rites in Western North America*, Anthropological Records Series (Berkeley: University of California Press, 1941). A general presentation of data supported by many maps and relevant to many of the topics considered in these chapters can be found in Harold E. Driver, *Indians of North America*, rev. ed. (Chicago: University of Chicago Press, 1969).

Also of value are the discussions of medicine and witchcraft in Virgil J. Vogel, *American Indian Medicine* (Norman: University of Oklahoma Press, 1970); and D. E. Walker, ed., *Systems of North American Witchcraft and Sorcery* (Moscow, Idaho: University Press of Idaho, 1970).

Chapter 6

Consult the Notes to this chapter for further readings relative to the specific examples presented. Of great value in studying the emergent religions in Native American histories is Harold W. Turner's extensive *Bibliography of New Religious Movements in Primal Societies*, vol. 2, *North America* (Boston: G. K. Hall, 1978). This bibliography includes almost 1,600 items organized by religious movement. The most valuable general interpretive study of these movements is that of Bryan R. Wilson, *Magic and the Millennium: A Sociological Study of Religious Movements of Protest among Tribal and Third-World Peoples* (New York: Harper & Row, 1973), which considers Native American examples along with those from many other cultures in the context of a broadly applicable sociological theory. Hazel W. Hertzberg's *The Search for an American Indian Identity: Modern Pan-Indian Movements* (Syracuse, N.Y.: Syracuse University Press, 1971) provides a broad historical consideration of this topic as well as specific histories of the most important movements. Deward E. Walker, ed., *The Emergent Native Americans: A Reader in Culture Contact* (Boston: Little, Brown, 1972) provides a wide-ranging selection of articles and bibliographies on this complex area of concern. Providing a view more from the perspective of Native American peoples is the collection of long essays by Edward H. Spicer, ed., *Perspectives in American Indian Culture Change* (Chicago: University of Chicago Press, 1961). As well as the Yaquis and Rio Grande Pueblos discussed in this chapter, this book considers the Mandan, Navajo, Wasco-Wishram, and Kwakiutl.

The single most notable observation I can make regarding further reading is that, compared to the abundance of primary material, so few interpretive works exist that are written from the perspective of the study of religion.

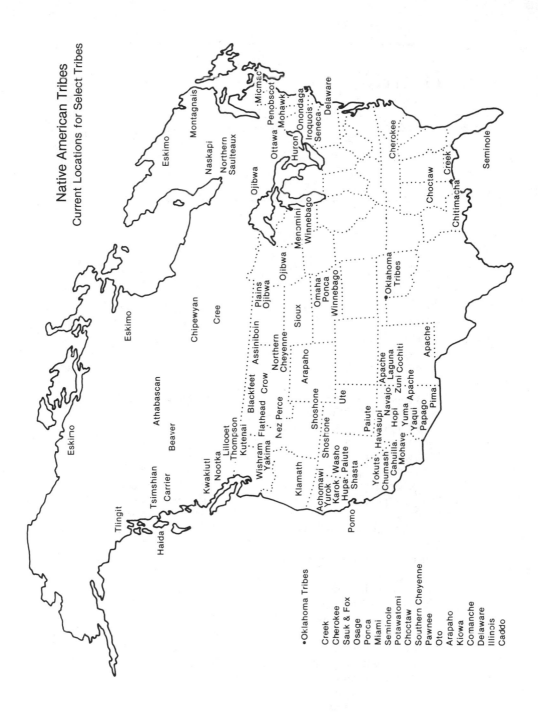

Native American Tribes
Current Locations for Select Tribes

• Oklahoma Tribes

Creek
Cherokee
Sauk & Fox
Osage
Ponca
Miami
Seminole
Potawatomi
Choctaw
Southern Cheyenne
Pawnee
Oto
Arapaho
Kiowa
Comanche
Delaware
Illinois
Caddo

Eskimo

Montagnais

Naskapi
Northern
Saulteaux

Micmac
Penobscot
Ottawa Mohawk
Huron Onondaga
Iroquois
Seneca
Delaware

Cherokee

Creek

Seminole

Choctaw

Chitimacha

Ojibwa

Menomini
Winnebago

Ojibwa

Plains
Ojibwa

Sioux

Omaha
Ponca
Winnebago

Oklahoma
Tribes

Cree

Chipewyan

Eskimo

Assinibion

Northern
Cheyenne

Arapaho

Apache
Navajo Laguna
Hopi Zuni Cochiti
Yuma Apache

Apache

Blackfeet Crow

Flathead
Nez Perce

Shoshone

Shoshone

Ute

Paiute

Papago Pima

Athabascan

Beaver

Kutenai
Lillooet
Thompson
Nootka

Kwakiutl

Wishram
Yakima

Klamath

Achomawi
Yurok
Karok Washo
Hupa Paiute
Shasta

Yokuts Havasupi
Chumash
Cahuilla
Mohave Yaqui
Yaqui

Pomo

Tlingit

Haida Tsimshian

Carrier

Eskino

Eskimo

Index